Contents

Summary

Arms fuel poverty and suffering

'It is like we are mopping the floor with the taps on. It takes five minutes to shower bullets, but it takes three hours and immense resources to repair each person.'

Dr Olive Kobusingye,
trauma surgeon in Uganda[3]

Every day, millions of men, women, and children are living in fear of armed violence. Every minute, one of them is killed. From the gangs of Rio de Janeiro and Los Angeles, to the civil wars of Liberia and Indonesia, arms are out of control.

The uncontrolled proliferation and misuse of arms by government forces and armed groups takes a massive human toll in lost lives, lost livelihoods, and lost opportunities to escape poverty. An average of US$22bn a year is spent on arms by countries in Africa, Asia, the Middle East, and Latin America – a sum that would otherwise enable those same countries to be on track to meet the Millennium Development Goals[4] of achieving universal primary education (estimated at $10bn a year) as well as targets for reducing infant and maternal mortality (estimated at $12bn a year).[5]

Every day in our work around the world, Oxfam and Amnesty International witness the abuse of arms which fuels conflict, poverty, and violations of human rights.

Arms are out of control

The impact of the widespread proliferation and misuse of arms is now critical. The 'war on terror' should have focused political will to prevent arms falling into the wrong hands. Instead, since the attacks on the World Trade Center and the Pentagon on 11 September 2001, some suppliers have relaxed their controls in order to arm new-found allies against 'terrorism', irrespective of their disregard for international human rights and humanitarian law. Despite the damage that they cause, there is still no binding, comprehensive, international law to control the export of conventional arms.

At the same time, we are seeing a long-term change, as guns are becoming an integral part of life – and therefore an increasingly common instrument of death – in more communities and cities around the world. From the pastoralists of northern Uganda to the gangs of Rio de Janeiro, the carrying and use of increasingly lethal weaponry is becoming the norm.

The time to act is now

Every government in the world has a responsibility to control arms – both their possession within its borders, to protect its own citizens, and their export across its borders, to ensure respect for international human rights and humanitarian law in the wider world. The world's most powerful governments, who are also the world's biggest arms suppliers, have the greatest responsibility to control the global trade. The five permanent members of the UN Security Council – France, Russia, China, the UK, and the USA – together account for 88 per cent of the world's conventional arms exports; and these exports contribute regularly to gross abuses of human rights.

The challenge to all governments is urgent. They must co-operate to control and limit the flow of arms and the spread of arms production. At the very least, arms-exporting countries must not supply arms where there is a clear danger that they will be used for violations of international human rights and humanitarian law. But to use the words of Olive Kobusingye, a surgeon treating the victims of gun violence in Uganda, it is not enough *either* to mop the floor *or* to turn off the tap – *both* the trade in arms and safety at community level must be addressed. Thus it is vital for communities directly affected by such violence to co-operate in removing lethal weapons. To achieve this, women, men, and children must be given protection by legitimate security forces which respect human rights.

To those who say that nothing can be done to control the flow of arms, Oxfam and Amnesty International argue that it can. The 1997 Landmines Treaty was brought into being by the combination of active governments and worldwide popular support. Although the scourge of landmines has not yet been eradicated, no country has openly traded in these weapons since 1997. The same combination of public pressure and action by sympathetic governments is needed to secure an Arms Trade Treaty.

Governments are acting too slowly to control arms. Amnesty International and Oxfam therefore propose urgent and interlinked action, from community level to international level, to control their proliferation and misuse more effectively.

▶ **International level** Governments are urged to agree an Arms Trade Treaty by 2006, to prevent arms being exported to destinations where they are likely to be used to commit grave violations of international human rights and humanitarian law.

▶ **Regional level** Governments are urged to develop and strengthen regional arms-control agreements to uphold international human rights and humanitarian law.

▶ **National level** Governments are urged to improve state capacity and their own accountability to control arms transfers and protect citizens from armed violence, in line with international laws and standards.

▶ **Community level** Civil society and local government agencies are urged to take effective action to improve safety at community level, by reducing the local availability and demand for arms.

Chapter 1
Arms – security for whom?

Children play on a burnt out Russian-made tank on the road to Shelab, Eritrea, a memorial to the end of Eritrea's liberation struggle with Ethiopia.

1: Arms – security for whom?

Too often, arms are misused.

▶ When used according to international law, arms can have a legitimate use. But too often they are used in ways that violate international human rights and humanitarian law.

▶ The availability of arms itself helps to fuel violence.

▶ This is powerfully demonstrated in the armed violence that occurs after conflicts have officially ended.

▶ Arms get into the wrong hands – be they abusive state security forces or other armed groups.

▶ More people are killed or injured by small arms than by heavy weapons.

The supply of weapons is an international problem with local consequences. Oxfam and Amnesty International are witnesses to widespread abuses of human rights, which are directly and indirectly attributable to the proliferation of weapons. From Côte d'Ivoire to Cambodia to Colombia, hundreds of thousands of people each year are unlawfully killed, and many more are injured by conventional weapons. The indirect consequences for human rights are even wider and deeper than this. Weapons in the wrong hands prevent access to hospitals, productive land, education, and markets, with short-term effects such as malnutrition and high rates of child mortality, as well as longer-term effects including illiteracy, higher risks of disease outbreaks, poverty, and poor governance. The culture of violence feeds upon itself. As conflict or lawlessness takes hold, countries slide into chaos, taking democracy and liberty hostage, and causing development to grind to a halt.

Whether used or not, weapons in the wrong hands do not give human rights and development a chance. They reduce the space for negotiating justice and peace, limiting incentives for co-operation, tolerance, and compromise. Trust is lost, and relationships are broken.

A limited role for arms

'The rule of the gun is the main obstacle to establishing peace.'

Hamid Karzai, President of the Transitional Administration in Afghanistan, November 2002[7]

Arms have a legitimate use in our society, but this use must be strictly controlled. States have the right to resort to arms to ensure that the life, liberty, and physical integrity of all their citizens are protected against external military attack, or imminent attack during internal law-enforcement operations. Stemming from this, arms can also play a specific role in international peace-keeping and peace-building operations. Many states exclusively retain the responsibility for protecting civilians and therefore do not encourage civilians to bear arms; some do not allow ordinary citizens to use certain arms.

However, neither states nor armed opposition groups have the right to use unlimited force. Stemming from a fundamental belief in the value of humanity, two significant bodies of international law seek to protect the individual (see Appendix 1).

▶ International human rights law is universal. It enshrines the principle of the right to life and security: everyone has the right not to be arbitrarily deprived of his or her life.

▶ International humanitarian law applies in situations of armed conflict. It seeks to regulate the conduct of war and reduce the suffering of civilians.

While the UN Charter legitimises a country's right to armed self-defence, it also applies principles of sustainable development to the use of arms, calling for the 'establishment and maintenance of international peace and security with the least diversion for armaments of the world's human and economic resources'. Yet with global military spending amounting to US$ 839bn a year,[8] the combination of 'over-armament and under-development', to quote a phrase first coined two decades ago, is still a real problem.

In peace and war, there are clear international legal principles defining how and when weapons can be employed, placing firm limits on their use.

Too many arms

In situations marred by armed conflict, crime, and state repression, the availability of arms itself is one important factor in determining the level of violence. The presence of arms can be a powerful catalyst in volatile scenarios.

The proliferation of arms facilitates the proliferation of armed violence. In an ever-downward spiral, the availability of arms can create a climate of fear: insecure groups and individuals arm themselves for protection, and their actions are perceived as a threat by others, who respond by arming themselves, and thus a demand for yet more weapons is created. Not only in times of war, but in 'peace time', the presence and availability of arms often intensifies violence engendered by political protest, disputes between neighbours, crime, and violence in the home. As weapons develop in sophistication – from stones, to bows and arrows, to automatic rifles – their lethality increases. A few well-armed individuals can cause death, injury, and fear on a massive scale. Killing becomes easier; it can be done from a longer range, with greater detachment and less effort.

The tragedies caused by irresponsible arms transfers

Afghanistan

Afghanistan has suffered 23 years of conflict, which have had a devastating effect on the country. The USA, as well as Pakistan, Iran, and China, played a key role in arming various forces fighting both against the Russians and against each other. The US supplied military aid to the Mujahideen in Afghanistan until 1991, despite the fact that thousands of Afghan civilians were being unlawfully killed, beaten, raped, and abducted.[10] Some of these supplies were subsequently used by the Taliban and the Northern Alliance – both of whom committed serious human rights abuses.

'First they rounded up the people in the streets. They then went from house to house and arrested the men of the families, except for the very old men. Nothing could stop them, and they did not spare any of the houses. In one house, the mother of a young man whom they were taking away held on to him, saying she would not allow him to go away without her. They began to hit the woman brutally with their rifle butts. She died. They took away the son and shot him dead. They executed a lot of people.' Testimony of a 15-year-old girl who was repeatedly raped by armed faction leaders in Kabul, Afghanistan, in 1994.[11]

Democratic Republic of the Congo (DRC)

More than three million civilians have been killed or have died from hunger and disease as a consequence of the conflict in the DRC (formerly Zaire) since August 1998. This conflict has been characterised by illegal killings, torture, and rape of civilians by forces on all sides. Despite this catalogue of human misery, many countries have continued to supply arms to the DRC.

The former Zairian government received arms from many countries, including Belgium, China, France, Germany, Israel, Spain, the United Kingdom (UK), and the USA. Deliveries of light weapons and associated military equipment from Albania, China, Egypt, Israel, Romania, Slovakia, South Africa and other countries, to the governments of Rwanda, Uganda, and Zimbabwe, have also been used in the conflict.[12]

In November 2001, around Kisangani, the scene of intense fighting involving many civilian deaths, Amnesty International found evidence of foreign military supplies in the form of ammunition cartridges for the following weapons: North Korean, Chinese, and Russian heavy machine guns, Russian revolvers, South African assault rifles, Chinese anti-aircraft weapons, and Russian, Bulgarian, or Slovak automatic grenade launchers.[13]

Supply routes and methods vary. British pilots and air cargo companies are not banned by the UK government from supplying weapons from overseas to armed forces in the DRC responsible for mass abuses of human rights. In addition, between 1993 and 1998, a time of rapidly escalating violent conflict and grave violations of human rights, Italy exported arms, munitions, and explosives worth nearly US$ 10m to the DRC.[14]

The danger of the sheer proliferation of arms can perhaps be best seen when war ends. Where weapons are still easily available, an end to violence remains as elusive as ever.

Arms in post-war violence

Too often, the problems facing countries after an armed conflict overwhelm them, and major violence erupts again: half of newly pacified countries revert to war within a decade.[16] Tackling the proliferation of arms is one vital step to help to prevent renewed outbreak of such armed conflicts.

Periods of extreme armed violence breed a culture of violence, whereby the influence and power of the military permeate into previously unaffected areas of society, and violence infects the symbols, attitudes, values, and beliefs that constitute 'culture'.[17] Crime and disorder increase,[18] driven principally by the legitimisation of violence,[19] coupled with the return of unemployed combatants and the easy availability of weapons. These weapons feed the systems of crime, smuggling, and organised violence which developed during periods of insecurity.

Studies demonstrate that if weapons are not removed and alternative viable livelihoods are not found, the risk of injury remains high, because the continued availability of weapons provides a violent means to resolve differences.

▶ Guatemala continues to be a very violent country. Although the Peace Accords were signed in 1996, a survey in 2000 found that 75 per cent of people felt that insecurity was increasing, and 88 per cent perceived a marked increase in the acquisition and proliferation of firearms.[20] Deaths from firearms increased from 69 per cent of all fatalities involving weapons in 1999 to 75 per cent in 2000, and firearms injuries increased from 52 to 60 per cent of all accidental injuries.[21]

▶ The number of people treated for firearms-related injuries at Monkol Borei Hospital in north-western Cambodia shows how the lack of effective disarmament contributes to a return to higher levels of violent conflict. There were 147 weapons injuries per 100,000 people just prior to the signing of the Peace Accord in 1991. During the transitional period under the control of the UN, the figure was 71 per 100,000. Five months after the UN had left, without fully disarming the population, the figure had risen to 163 per 100,000 people.[22]

It stands to reason, therefore, that demobilisation, disarmament, and reintegration programmes are a necessity after the official end of armed conflict. Countries are often flooded with armed former fighters; surplus arms must be taken out of the

'There is a universal understanding that if weapons are present it will lead to conflict.'

Mervyn Patterson, the UN's chief representative in northern Afghanistan, working with local leaders on security, 2002[15]

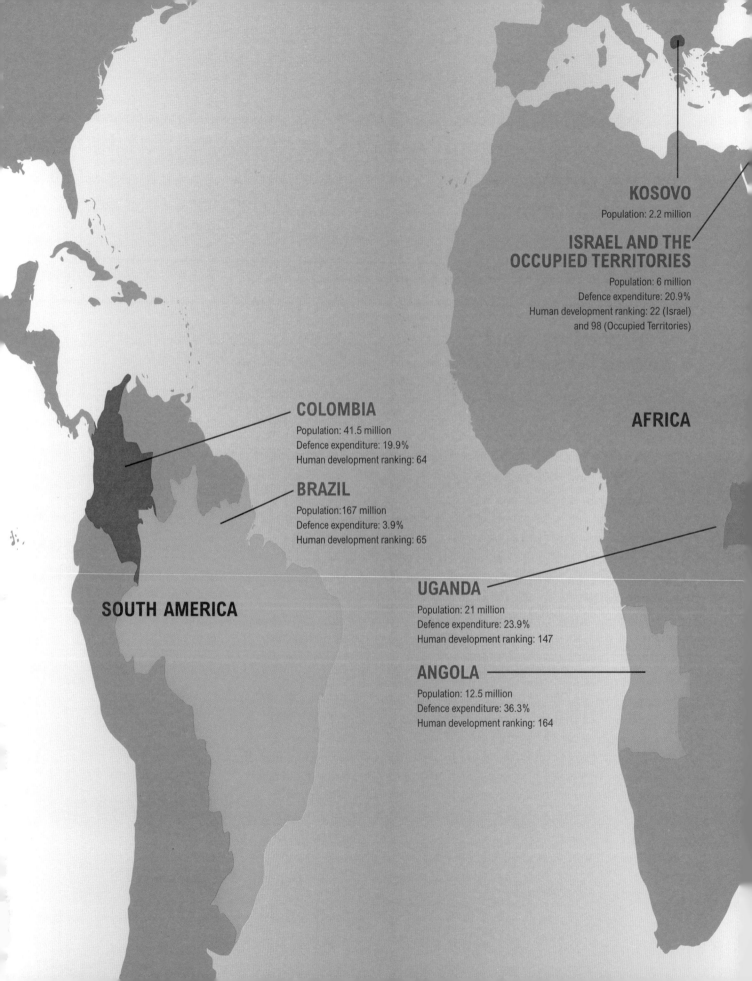

KOSOVO

Population: 2.2 million

**ISRAEL AND THE
OCCUPIED TERRITORIES**

Population: 6 million
Defence expenditure: 20.9%
Human development ranking: 22 (Israel)
and 98 (Occupied Territories)

AFRICA

COLOMBIA

Population: 41.5 million
Defence expenditure: 19.9%
Human development ranking: 64

BRAZIL

Population: 167 million
Defence expenditure: 3.9%
Human development ranking: 65

UGANDA

Population: 21 million
Defence expenditure: 23.9%
Human development ranking: 147

SOUTH AMERICA

ANGOLA

Population: 12.5 million
Defence expenditure: 36.3%
Human development ranking: 164

Photo: Tiago Quiroga/Viva Rio

Brazil

Sixteen-year-old Camila Magalhães Lima lost the use of her legs in 1998 when she was hit by a stray bullet in a shoot-out between thieves and private security forces while walking home from school.[27]

'I had plans for the future; I wanted to travel the world, take a modelling course, and continue my gymnastics training. From one day to the next, my dreams were shattered – all because of the irresponsibility of supposedly civilised men who only feel brave with a gun in their hands.'

Photograph blurred for personal safety reasons

Colombia

Marcos from a rural community in Urabá, Colombia

'They [the paramilitaries] began to bother us, pressuring us to inform on the guerrillas. When we go to town to buy supplies, the paramilitaries accuse us of supplying the guerrillas. The guerrillas have been passing through the area for years. We don't carry guns. All we want to do is to plant our crops, take care of our animals, and manage the river and forest.'[30]

▲ In the last 10 years, 300,000 people have been killed in Brazil, many as a result of urban violence and the widespread proliferation of handguns and small arms, which account for 63 per cent of all homicides in Brazil.[28] Many of the weapons are made in Brazil, but guns are also imported from foreign countries – in order of importance, from the USA, Spain, Belgium, Germany, Italy, the Czech Republic, Austria, and France.[29]

▲ Colombia's conflict has been marked by the violation of human rights by all sides. There have been increases in the supply of arms to guerrillas, including large shipments from Peru and Venezuela, in addition to the arms that have found their way into the country from other anti-government forces in Latin America over many years.[31] Large quantities of small arms have also been supplied, in the last few years, to the Colombian authorities by the USA, France, Germany, Spain, and South Africa.[32]

The human cost

Photo: Howard Davies/Oxfam

Cambodia

Yem Para, from Phnom Penh, Cambodia.[23]

Yem Para was shot several times by someone known to her. 'One day we argued. I was with some other people, planting vegetables, and he shot me through the leg – my left leg, here above the knee. Then he shot me through the chest, and the third bullet just skimmed my hair, it was so close. He used an AK-47 and was only about 20 metres away, and then came closer. At first everyone was afraid to intervene, but when he'd finished the rounds, the neighbours came and stopped him bashing me with the butt of the gun. I still get pain from my wounds. I only had the metal pin out of my leg five months ago. And now I can only do about half what I used to. Before, I could lift 50kg of rice, but now I can only lift about 10kg.'

▲ Covert arms shipments from China and the USA to Cambodia's anti-Vietnamese factions began in the late 1970s. Around 500,000 small arms are believed to remain in Cambodia – half of them controlled by the official military and police forces and half by militiamen, demobilised soldiers, and other individuals.[24]

Photo: Islands Business

Solomon Islands

Sir Fred Soaki, highly respected former Solomon Islands Police Commissioner and leading member of the Peace Monitoring Group, was assassinated on 10 February 2003 while eating in a restaurant. He was renowned for his neutrality and his fearless confrontation of rogue police officers and former militants in his attempts to persuade them to give up their guns under a UNDP-assisted programme. The suspected killer, a police officer, was arrested but escaped from custody.[25]

▲ Militias which had used old World War II rifles and home-made shotguns raided barely protected police stores in the Solomon Islands to gain access to high-powered assault rifles. Many of these rifles were supplied from Singapore. Australia has previously refused weapons sales to the Solomon Islands, concerned about their potential impact on the peace process. The USA agreed to ship arms costing US$ 4m in 1997, but these were impounded by Australia and New Zealand, at the request of the newly elected government in the Solomon Islands.[26]

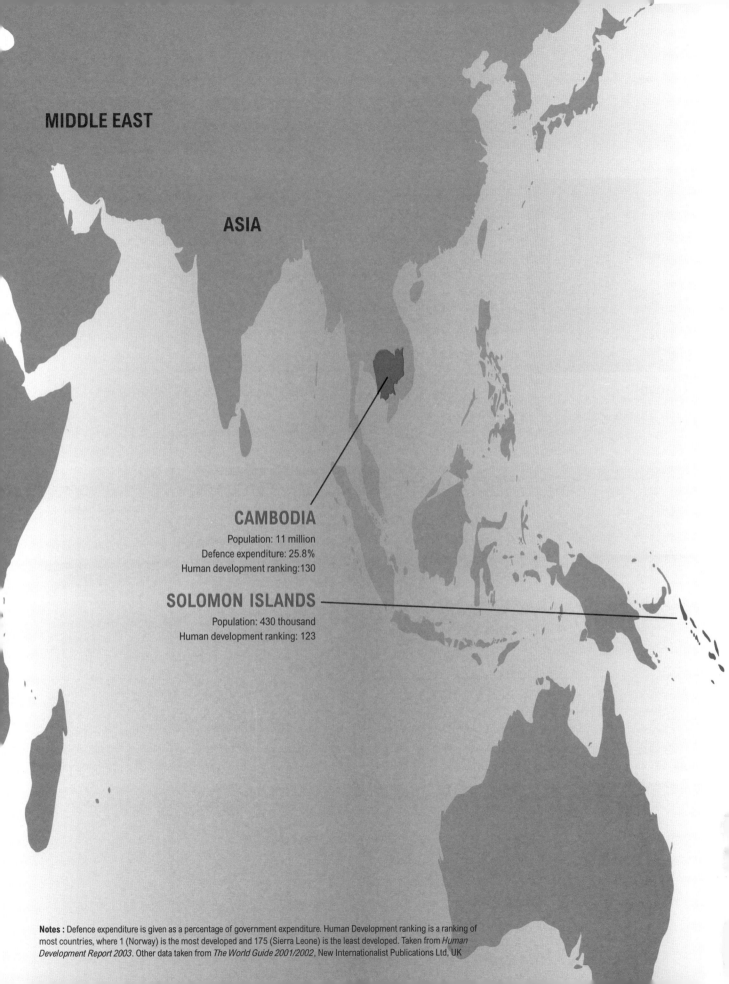

MIDDLE EAST

ASIA

CAMBODIA

Population: 11 million
Defence expenditure: 25.8%
Human development ranking:130

SOLOMON ISLANDS

Population: 430 thousand
Human development ranking: 123

Notes : Defence expenditure is given as a percentage of government expenditure. Human Development ranking is a ranking of most countries, where 1 (Norway) is the most developed and 175 (Sierra Leone) is the least developed. Taken from *Human Development Report 2003*. Other data taken from *The World Guide 2001/2002*, New Internationalist Publications Ltd, UK

Oxfam Photo

Kosovo

Petrija Piljevic, a 57-year old Serb woman living in Kosovo, was abducted by three men wearing uniforms of the Kosovo Liberation Army (KLA) on 28 June 1999. Her neighbours saw her being taken from her flat in Priština/Prishtina, crying and screaming. When her body was returned to her family in August 2001, it was reported that she had been shot twice at close range in the chest. This killing was one of a pattern of gross human rights abuses committed by members of the KLA and Serb forces in the Kosovo conflict.

▲ In the late 1990s, substantial weapons trafficking in the Balkans was organised by ethnic Albanian armed opposition groups and their supporters, particularly in the ethnic Albanian diaspora communities of Germany, Austria, and Switzerland.[37] The weapons networks developed from the mid-1990s onwards and have spread small arms throughout ethnic Albanian communities in Kosovo, the Former Yugoslav Republic of Macedonia, and southern Serbia for use by ethnic Albanian armed opposition groups. According to one report in 1999, Macedonian police estimated that anywhere between 20,000 and 30,000 small arms were cached in the western part of the country by KLA operatives and sympathisers.[38]

Photo: AP

Israel and the Occupied Territories

A vicious cycle of armed violence has gripped Israel and the Occupied Territories since the recent *intifada* began in September 2000. Since the start of the *intifada*, more than 2,100 Palestinians have been killed by the Israeli army, including some 380 children; Palestinian armed groups have killed some 750 Israelis, most of them civilians, and including more than 90 children.[39] In one case, on 10 October 2000, eleven-year-old Sami Fathi Abu Jazzar, pictured above, was fatally wounded in the head, and six other Palestinians were injured when Israeli soldiers opened fire on a crowd of some 400 people, mainly schoolchildren. Three weeks later, an Israeli man and woman were killed and ten bystanders were injured when a car packed with explosives blew up in a side street in central Jerusalem's Mahane Yehuda market.[40]

▲ The arms used by Palestinian armed groups come from a variety of sources; mortars appear to be home-made; some are apparently smuggled in from Jordan and Egypt; and some, according to local police sources, are bought from Israeli illicit small-arms traders.[41] Israel, as well as producing its own arms, including the Galil assault rifle and Uzi machine gun, was the largest recipient during the 1990s of US-exported military rifles, including M-16s.[42]

Photo: Crispin Hughes/Oxfam

Angola

Rodrina Faustina, aged 42, in a camp for displaced people near Kuito, Angola.[33]

'This isn't the first time UNITA *[União Nacional para a Independência Total de Angola]* has attacked. In October 1990 they came to the village, stealing things. I tried to escape, but they shot me in the leg. I got first aid, then I was brought to the hospital here in Kuito, and they had to amputate my leg below the knee... We stayed in Kuito for three years, then went back to our village. There are so many things that I find difficult now... To go to the river with a bucket of washing on crutches is very difficult. Also to go and cut wood for cooking to help my husband. Washing clothes, washing dishes, fetching water: all these things are hard.'

▲ During the Cold War, South Africa, Portugal, and NATO countries developed strategies to supply and sponsor UNITA covertly. The networks and many of the brokers and traffickers continued to supply UNITA in the 1990s, despite a UN arms embargo. The main supply routes were through South Africa, Burkina Faso, the Democratic Republic of Congo (former Zaire), Republic of Congo (Congo-Brazzaville), Zambia, and Namibia – with or without government complicity, and often with the involvement of European nationals.[34]

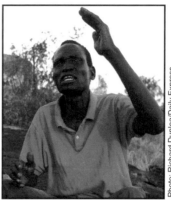

Photo: Richard Dunlea/Daily Express

Uganda

Charles Logwe, aged 46, from Uganda used to buy small numbers of weapons in Sudan and sell them in Uganda. On one expedition he bought 12 guns, four for himself and eight for others, and made good money by selling his haul.

'It is very easy. Karamojong and Acholi marry Sudanese and vice versa, so there is always someone with a reason to go back and forth.'

Then his uncle and brother were shot in an ambush, and his brother lost a leg. 'When I saw them and others with such terrible wounds all over their bodies, it gave me a lot of thought and sorrow, and I knew I could not trade in guns again.'[35]

▲ The government of Sudan has been an extremely important source of weapons for the Lord's Resistance Army (LRA), a rebel group in northern Uganda, providing AK-47 and G3 assault rifles, anti-tank weaponry (including B10 recoilless guns), 81 mm and 82 mm mortars, and landmines.[36] In 2002, the Sudanese government stopped supporting the LRA, in return for the Ugandan government's agreement to end its support for Sudanese rebels.

hands of former fighters; these arms should be destroyed, and livelihoods must be restored. In June 2003, there were thought to be 24 million guns in Iraq, enough to arm every man, woman, and child, and they could be purchased for around US$ 10 each; this has been one factor in the state of insecurity and acts of lawlessness still prevailing in the country.[44]

It is not only small arms that are left behind. Landmines, bomblets from cluster bombs, and other unexploded ordnance (UXO) remain well after the official end of conflict, causing between 15,000 and 20,000 new casualties each year, with huge loss of life and permanent disability. Cluster bombs have been a major source of death and injury in Iraq. The presence of landmines and UXO inhibits access to homes and fields, preventing people from restarting their lives and rebuilding their country.[45]

Arms in the wrong hands

If weapons in too many hands risk increasing violence, weapons in the wrong hands pose an even greater risk that they will be used to abuse human rights.

In 2002, there were over 40 situations of conflict involving armed violence of varying intensity around the world.[46] In virtually all of these conflicts, the forces involved – be they state forces or armed groups – are responsible for abusing international human rights and humanitarian law. But state forces in peacetime often also use their authorised weapons for abuse. Law-enforcement officials are invested with power and equipped with weapons, but in some countries they are paid wages that barely cover their subsistence needs. Often they receive limited training, and sometimes none at all. In some countries, armed extortion and corruption on the part of security forces and law enforcers is rife and goes unpunished by corrupt judicial systems.

Laws, regulations, and training courses for police and other law enforcers often ignore the elementary rules agreed internationally for their conduct – including the UN Basic Principles on the Use of Force and Firearms by Law Enforcement Officials, the UN Code of Conduct for Law Enforcement Officials, and the UN Standard Minimum Rules for the Treatment of Prisoners.[47] In South Africa, nearly 100,000 security officers had not been trained for the level of work they undertook; in 1999, three quarters of all security officers had only the lowest-grade qualifications, which enabled officers to be armed and deployed after only five hours of firearms training.[48]

In Timor Leste (East Timor), the rapid development of a professional police service after the end of the long years of conflict was recognised as a key goal. However, police training has been inadequate, and effective oversight and accountability mechanisms are lacking. Complaints of assaults and excessive use of force by police are increasing. In December 2002, for example, two people were shot dead and 16 others were injured in the capital, Dili, when police reportedly used excessive force against rioters. Police officers have been issued with pepper spray, batons, and Austrian Glock pistols, and there are plans to issue a selected number of officers in the Rapid Intervention Units with German-designed MP5 sub-machine guns.[49]

Throughout Latin America, the rapid growth and increasing power of private security companies is a real concern. According to the Guatemalan government, there are about 116 private security companies operating in the country, employing 35,000 agents: an unofficial force greater than the entire army, and twice the number of police officers.[50] In El Salvador, fewer than half of the 17,000 private security agents had done a five-day training course as required by law.[51]

International arms supplies to those responsible for gross human rights abuses send a message that the behaviour of such groups is tolerated, even supported, by the international community. Weapons shipments to such abusers of human rights may actually encourage further atrocities by reinforcing the impunity with which they operate.

The particular role of small arms

Although this report addresses the need to control all conventional weapons, it should be emphasised that small arms have a particular role to play in contributing to poverty and suffering. Small arms are present in every country of the world. They are used in every single conflict – and used exclusively in most. They play a key role in perpetrating abuses of international human rights and humanitarian law – through their direct use or through the threat of use. More injuries, deaths, displacements, rapes, kidnappings, and acts of torture are inflicted or perpetrated with small arms than with any other type of weapon. In Colombia, it is estimated that nine out of ten atrocities committed against civilians by all armed groups involve the use of small arms.[53]

There are approximately 639 million small arms in the world today, produced by more than 1,135 companies in at least 98 countries. Eight million new weapons are produced every year. Nearly 60 per cent of small arms are in civilian hands.[54] At least 16 billion units of military ammunition were produced in 2001 alone –more than two military bullets for every man, woman, and child on the planet.[55]

The Kalashnikov is the godfather of assault rifles. Total production is estimated to be between 70 and 100 million, comprising up to 80 per cent of the total number of assault rifles in the world.[52]

Who possesses the world's small arms?

Source: Small Arms Survey 2002, data from 31.12.01

Privately owned

59.2%

378.3m*

Government armed forces

37.8%

241.6m

Police
2.8%

18m

Armed opposition groups

0.2%

1m

Total 638.9 million
*Millions of guns

Small arms are light, easy to operate, and – obviously – lethal.

▶ Handguns are small enough to fit in a pocket, inexpensive, and often widely available. Some small guns in the USA are so cheap and easily concealable that they are called 'Saturday Night Specials'; these are typically small, around .25-calibre, and can be bought for as little as US$ 75. Police often use 9 mm pistols, which can shoot accurately over a distance of some 50 metres, and semi-automatic carbines, which are supposed to shoot accurately over 200 metres. However, in many countries police and paramilitaries carry much more dangerous high-velocity assault rifles, such as AK-47s.

▶ Assault rifles are simple and durable, with only a few moving parts; their use requires little training, and they can remain operational for 20–40 years or more, with only minimal maintenance. They are also highly portable, easily concealed, and relatively cheap. An AK-47 fires up to 30 rounds in less than three seconds, with each bullet potentially lethal at distances exceeding one kilometre.

▶ Shoulder-fired rocket launchers and portable air-defence systems can be operated by only two people. They have an overwhelming destructive power. Some are 'fire and forget' missiles, finding their target by infra-red systems, with a range of between one and eight kilometres. They include the US-made Stinger missile systems, used to devastating effect in Afghanistan, and the Strela missile, which was fired at (but missed) an Israeli civilian airliner in Kenya in November 2002. The simpler rocket launchers, such as the Russian RPG-7, can bring down helicopters and penetrate tank armour 330 mm thick at distances of up to 500 metres.

Small arms are so prevalent that it is estimated that there is one such weapon for every 10 people – men, women, and children – in the world. Numbers vary widely even within regions: from 5.8 people per gun in Pakistan, to 180 in Bangladesh.[57]

Top four assault rifles in the world

AK-47/74 (Russia)   **70-100 million**

M-16 (USA)   **7 million**

G3 (Germany)   **7 million**

FAL (Belgium)   **5-7 million**

The country named is the original manufacturer – these weapons are now produced in many other countries.
Source: Small Arms Survey 2001

24

Bacary Biaye in a small ward at the Regional Hospital in Ziguinchor, Casamance, Senegal.
He was shot in July 1999 during a rebel attack on a bus, and has lost the use of his legs.

2: The human cost of arms abuse

The real cost of arms is much too high.

▶ In our work, Amnesty International and Oxfam are witnesses to the use of arms to commit gross abuses of international human rights and humanitarian law – whether in conflict, crime, law enforcement, state repression, or violence in the home.

▶ The misuse of arms jeopardises people's fundamental rights, including the right to life.

▶ The indirect effects, often overlooked, are huge. Arms are misused to deny people access to land, markets, schools, and hospitals, and thus contribute to increases in malnutrition and disease.

▶ In the long term, these effects increase poverty and derail development.

Arms are one key factor in facilitating, prolonging, and intensifying conflict and armed violence. Arms are used arbitrarily and indiscriminately to kill or injure, to threaten people and drive them from their homes; the flow of arms enables and sustains conflicts in which civilian casualties mount. At a deeper level, the misuse of arms may obstruct the possibilities for development and interfere with people's rights to a decent livelihood, health services, and education.

More than 500,000 civilians are estimated to die each year on average from the misuse of conventional arms: one person every minute.[59]

The right to life

In the time taken to read this page, one more person will most likely be killed somewhere in the world, and at least two more will have been seriously injured by the use of arms.

Armed conflict: the easy availability of arms tends to increase the incidence of armed violence, prolong wars once they break out, and enable grave and widespread abuses of human rights.[60] In some situations, the escalating supply of arms acts as a *trigger* for conflict. For example, arms shipments to Rwanda, principally from China, France, South Africa, and Egypt, in the tense months preceding the civil war in Rwanda in 1994, are widely considered to have encouraged and facilitated the eventual genocide, even though most atrocities were committed by people wielding agricultural tools.[61] The importance of arms is greatest as *fuel* to sustain long-term conflict, responsible not so much for the initiation of wars, but for their continuation. Armed conflicts cannot be sustained without the supply of arms or, where they are already abundant, without ammunition.[62] For example, attack helicopters provided by German and Belgian arms brokers were used in 1997 by government forces to strafe the residential areas of Brazzaville, Republic of Congo, killing thousands of civilians.[64]

After one bombing raid by the US-led Coalition in Iraq using cluster bombs at al-Hilla, more than 200 people were wounded, about 80 per cent of whom were civilians. One eyewitness described how 'the wounds were vicious and deep, a rash of scarlet spots on the back and thighs or face, the shards of shrapnel from the cluster bombs buried an inch or more in the flesh... Patients reported that explosives fell "like grapes" from the sky'.[65]

Beyond armed conflicts: in crime-ridden societies, the easy availability of arms is linked to the level of armed violence.[66] While there is debate over the best way of ameliorating the culture of violence that is often prevalent in such societies, this basic concern cannot be ignored. Studies from developed countries (data are rarely available elsewhere) consistently show a clear correlation between household gun ownership and death rates. This link is most clearly seen in the case of suicides and accidental deaths, and especially among young people.[67] Sometimes it is police and other law-enforcement officials who commit armed crime and violate human rights. In Brazil, police in many areas have been linked to 'death squads' responsible for hundreds of killings, including those of children, which have long gone unpunished. Federal investigations in 2002 indicated that all branches of the *Espírito Santo* state authorities had been infiltrated by organised criminals, with consequent increases in systematic violations of human rights, including summary executions by police.[68]

Poor people are more likely than rich people to fall victim to violent crime
Source: US National Criminal Victimization Survey, 2001.

Figures:
Top: Violent crimes per 1,000 people (aged 12 or over)
Bottom: Family income of victims

| 46.6 | 36.9 | 31.8 | 29.1 | 26.3 | 21 | 18.5 |

| Less than $7,500 | $7,500 to $14,999 | $15,000 to $24,999 | $25,000 to $34,999 | $35,000 to $49,999 | $50,000 to $74,999 | $75,000 and above |

'I saw bodies on the ground as I ran with my children. The [helicopter] gunships were shooting at us, so I could not stop to see if they were alive. The gunships also fired rockets that set the village on fire.'

Yak Gatdet Kok, from Nhialdiu in southern Sudan, 2001[63]

'The bombing was very severe. They mainly hit military targets, but the force of the explosions was so intense. It was terrible for children and people with heart problems. My children used to rush to me, I could feel their hearts pounding like a little bird in your hand.'

Gholam Rassoul, a driver in Herat, Afghanistan, 2002[69]

The number of deaths from small arms varies hugely between different countries, from 0.01 deaths per 100,000 people in Hong Kong, to 30 per 100,000 in El Salvador, to 55 per 100,000 in Colombia. Risks also vary within countries: the average firearm-homicide rate in Kenya as a whole, for example, is 10–15 per 100,000 people, whereas in the north-east and north-west of the country, where arms are widely available, the rate climbs to 580 per 100,000.[70] Such statistics cannot convey the reality of the human suffering caused by these weapons.

▶ It is men, especially young men, who are the most common perpetrators and the most common victims of gun violence, in times of both war and 'peace'. In Rio de Janeiro, Brazil, young men are 24 times more likely than women to be killed by firearms; in Colombia they are 14 times more likely to die of gunshot wounds.[71]

▶ Nevertheless, women have been killed and injured in great numbers by shooting and bombing in armed conflict. Women and girls made up a high proportion of the victims when armed forces drove hundreds of thousands of refugees from camps in the Great Lakes Region in 1996 and deliberately executed refugees en masse.[72]

▶ The young are not spared. Children have become targets in drug wars, in political and gang-related killing, in civil and international wars, and as victims of police brutality. In Honduras, at least 1,817 street children have been killed over the last five years.[73] Interviews with a group of Croatian refugee children in 1992 revealed that 85 per cent had experienced shooting, 67 per cent shelling, and 24 per cent bombing.[74]

▶ Nor are older people spared. In Kosovo from February 1998 to June 1999, the mortality rate from armed violence for men aged 50 or over was nearly 10 times that of women from the same age group, and more than three times that of men of military age (15–49 years), which suggests that Serb forces may have been specifically targeting the traditional heads of households in order to weaken the social and cultural integrity of local society.[75]

The death and injury of such large numbers of people, many young, have profound consequences for development: reducing the number of people entering the work force, diverting family and social resources into the care of those disabled by gun violence, and forcing governments to redirect funding from social services to public security.[76]

Violations of civil and political rights

Arms are frequently used for direct violations of the rights to life and to physical and mental integrity, but they are also the means through which coercion can be brought to bear to perpetrate any number of other abuses. The threatening use of arms by security forces, armed groups, or others in positions of authority places those subject to their control in a very vulnerable position, often literally at their mercy.

Torture and arbitrary arrests

Violations take place while people are detained, either in police stations, detention centres, or prisons. The statistics are shocking. Between 1997 and 2000, Amnesty International received reports of torture or ill-treatment by state officials in more than 150 countries. In more than 70, the offences were widespread or persistent. In more than 80 countries, people reportedly died as a result of their treatment at the hands of those in authority. The evidence strongly suggests that most of the victims were people suspected or convicted of criminal offences. Most of the torturers were police officers who used armed threats and violence to subdue their victims.[80]

Sometimes torturers use weapons that are supposed to be 'safer' than traditional firearms: 'We saw them shock the [Haitian] detainee on his body with an electric shield, also with an electric gun. ...The Haitian detainee was shocked about three times. While being shocked, the Haitian detainee was handcuffed, his hands to his legs, lying on his side on the floor.' This testimony was one of many disturbing allegations of torture or ill-treatment made by people detained by the US Immigration and Naturalization Service and held at the Jackson County Correctional Facility, Florida between August 1997 and July 1998.[81]

Sexual violence

Armed sexual violence is horrifically widespread in heavily armed environments. Weapons can be used to facilitate systematic rape – a war crime, used to hasten the expulsion of national groups by degrading women and spreading terror, fear, and humiliation. Sexual violence against men may also be significant, but few data on this type of abuse have so far been collated, and it is believed that most cases are not reported.

Women and girls are raped at gunpoint while away from home collecting firewood and water, or undertaking other daily tasks; they are also vulnerable in jail or refugee

'They started beating me, and terrorising me with a Kalashnikov. They put a tyre around my neck and told me they would burn me if I did not confess. I confessed, but it wasn't true.'

Samuel Nsengiyumva, aged 14, arrested in Burundi and accused of stealing a soldier's gun[79]

camps, with no place to hide. At least 15,700 women and girls in Rwanda and 25,000 in Croatia and Bosnia are reported to have been raped at times of armed conflict; the actual figures may be much higher.[83] This can have implications for HIV/AIDS infection: soldiers often have a much higher infection rate than the civilian population, and forced sex is more likely to lead to transmission.[84]

Violence in the home, sometimes armed, by intimate partners and friends increases during conflict, as sanctions against men's violence break down, and women's social and economic vulnerability increases.[85] Threatening behaviours are astonishingly similar across cultures: they include shooting the family dog as a warning, or getting out a gun and cleaning it during an argument.[86] Forty per cent of women contacting the SOS Hotline in Belgrade during the war in the former Yugoslavia said they had been threatened with weapons, and a 10-month study in Northern Ireland showed that the increased availability of guns meant that more dangerous forms of violence were used against women in the home.[87]

In non-conflict situations, a number of studies have suggested that the risk of being murdered by an intimate partner increases with the availability of firearms.[88] Where they are readily available, firearms are the weapons of choice when men kill their partners. In the USA, 51 per cent of female murder victims are shot, according to the Violence Policy Center in 1999. Consistent with other international studies, research by the Gun Control Alliance in South Africa in 1999 suggests that more women are shot at home in acts of domestic violence than are shot by strangers on the streets or by intruders.

The psychological impact

Physical injuries command most attention, yet the psychological burden of armed attack is severe and enduring, though frequently overlooked. Psychiatrists in Croatia working with women who have been raped, bereaved, or displaced, believe that it will take two to three generations before the psychological effects of the war pass.[90] Four out of five women raped in 1994 in Rwanda continue to suffer psychological trauma.[91]

Ex-combatants may display panic attacks and aggressive behaviour,[92] as well as despair and helplessness as a result of their inability to provide for and protect their families. Children have their own particular psychological burdens, which are often barely addressed.[93] A UNICEF-funded survey found that 75 per cent of the children in the Occupied Territories were suffering emotional problems from their experience of the conflict, with repeated exposure to the sound of shelling and shooting cited as the major cause of psychological damage.[94]

Forced to flee

At the end of 2002, around 22 million people across the world were internally displaced. About 13 million were refugees and asylum-seekers seeking protection outside their own countries.[96] Most of the world's displaced population consists of women and children.[97] Estimates show that 4.3 million people were newly uprooted in 2002, the majority in Africa.[98] In Sudan, more than four million people are displaced; 85 per cent of the inhabitants of southern Sudan are thought to have been displaced at least once in the last 15 years.[99] In Colombia, more than 250,000 people have been displaced each year for the last five years – in 2002, the figure was estimated to be 350,000.[100]

In other places, armed groups and governments put limits on people's movement: checkpoints prevent free passage, borders are closed, passes are required, civilians are 'advised' when to travel. These restrictions bar access to food, work, basic commerce, education, and medical attention. The right to move freely is particularly critical for pregnant women, and sick and injured people.

Those who find themselves in refugee camps may not see an end to fear and armed violence, because many camps have become increasingly militarised. They are sometimes used as hubs for arms trafficking (for example, Dadaab camp in north-eastern Kenya, used as a reception point for arms arriving from Somalia); or they are used as a source of recruitment for rebel forces (for example, camps in West and Central Africa). Too often, governments and the international community have failed to minimise this risk by providing adequate protection for refugees.

In mid-2000, Guinea hosted some 350,000 Sierra Leonean and 150,000 Liberian refugees who had fled the conflicts in their respective countries. From September 2000, however, with a total breakdown of security along the three borders, Guinea changed from a place of refuge to a place of violence. According to Amnesty International, refugee camps throughout the country were attacked by armed political groups, and countless refugees were killed, beaten, raped, tortured, and abducted as they fled from one camp to another, trying to stay ahead of the violence. Others were arrested, tortured or killed by the security forces. As they travelled, they faced military or civilian checkpoints and roadblocks, where they were humiliated, threatened, and forced to pay bribes or hand over food and other possessions. Refugees fleeing on foot from one camp to another had to pass so many checkpoints that they literally had no money or possessions left. In at least one incident, helicopter gunships flew low over a refugee camp and launched artillery close to the camp, resulting in civilian deaths and injuries, in attacks which appeared to be an attempt to frighten the refugees into leaving.[101]

'When the planes first started to fly over us, we thought it was just a display. But then they started dropping bombs near us. We were surprised and we were scared. Everyone ran for their lives. All their property, whatever they owned, was left behind. We didn't know where some family members were. We found each other at this evacuation centre.'

Male resident of an evacuation centre in Pagalungan, Mindanao, Philippines[95]

One neglected reality is the connection between arms sales and the displacement of thousands of people as a consequence of human rights abuses. Governments in wealthier countries may be willing to sell arms to countries committing gross violations of human rights, yet they rarely welcome asylum-seekers from those same countries. In the European Union (EU), more than one million asylum applications were lodged between 2000 and 2002; the highest number came from Iraq, followed by the Federal Republic of Yugoslavia, Afghanistan, and Turkey.[103] Armed forces in all these countries received arms from EU states during the 1980s and 1990s.[104]

Abduction and hostage-taking

Men, women, and children are abducted at gunpoint and forced to fight or work for their abductors. In Uganda, the Lord's Resistance Army has abducted more than 20,000 children since 1986; children make up a very high proportion of LRA soldiers. Those caught trying to escape are summarily executed, as a warning to others.[106] Between 10,000 and 17,000 women and children have been abducted from southern Sudan; as recently as early 2003, government and allied militia abducted civilian men and boys for military purposes, while women and children were taken to government-controlled towns in the oilfields around Bentiu, where the women were forced to provide manual labour and sexual services.[107]

Civilians are also taken hostage and held for ransom by armed forces. Guerrilla groups and paramilitaries kidnapped more than 1,400 people during 2002 in Colombia.[108]

'Disappearances'

Small arms are used in thousands of 'disappearances' all over the world. People are captured by government forces or their paramilitary allies, who then deny all knowledge of the detainees. Most of them are feared dead, the victims of extra-judicial executions. Their families face the often prolonged agony of not knowing what has happened to their loved ones.

The world has recently seen evidence of the horrific scale of such abuses in Iraq. In Chechnya, it was reckoned that at least 540 Chechens had gone missing without trace since the beginning of the second conflict in 1999 until 2001;[109] the fate and whereabouts of approximately 20,000 people in the former Yugoslavia remain unknown to this day.[110]

Silencing opposition

Political activists, journalists, trade unionists, and peaceful demonstrators are frequently attacked by government or other armed forces seeking to deprive them of their freedom of expression and association. Trade unionists in Colombia have been threatened, attacked, and assassinated, and have 'disappeared'. Most of those responsible for these abuses have not been punished. Between 1 January and 15 October 2002, 118 trade unionists were killed.[111] Arms are also used by government forces, their proxies, or other political groups to suppress pressure for democratic change; they thus do particular harm to democracy and good governance. In 2002, violence marred the period leading to the Zimbabwean local elections in September;[112] and approximately 732 people were killed in Kashmir from the announcement of the polls to their close in October.[113]

Violations of social and economic rights

International law recognises that states share responsibilities for the protection and fulfilment of basic economic and social rights. Where states transfer weapons to countries in the knowledge that doing so is likely to set back efforts to meet the needs for health care, education, housing, or a basic standard of living – all of which are fundamental human rights – they may contribute to the continuing denial of these rights.

Denial of aid

Armed violence, actual and threatened, prevents aid reaching those who desperately need it. Warring parties may purposely block humanitarian assistance, using access to food and medical supplies as a military tactic. Sometimes aid workers, their convoys, their offices, and their programmes are specifically targeted. One hundred and eighty civilian aid workers were killed in acts of violence between 1997 and 2001, the greatest proportion of whom died as a result of ambushes of vehicles, carried out by bandits or rebel groups.[116] One of the key responses to this type of danger is to suspend both humanitarian and development programmes and withdraw aid workers, thus denying the delivery of aid to needy communities.

In the year 2001–2, Oxfam GB temporarily suspended emergency assistance programmes in nine countries, withdrew key management staff twice, had staff hospitalised twice, and completely closed one programme, in addition to taking many other security precautions. The suspension, even if temporary, of a relief

'Life has changed completely due to the war. Our schools have been closed.
Now the closest school is about 12 miles away.
As a result, many have dropped out of school.
Now we do not do our harvesting and other cultivation work without consulting the police.
In the past we had cultivators' meetings to decide on these matters, now we have meetings with the police!'
Villager from Welikanda, Sri Lanka, 1998[114]

Indonesia, the second highest recipient of net overseas aid, spends almost the same sum of money on its military forces as it receives in aid.[115]

programme delivering food, water, sanitation, or basic health products has obvious and direct effects. Equally important is the loss of protection: as aid agencies withdraw, both civilians and military forces know that witnesses from the international community have left, no longer able to testify to any violations of international human rights or humanitarian law.

Armed violence hinders the arrival of aid and affects mechanisms for the provision of aid. In the mid-1980s a disastrous drought struck much of Africa, and on-going wars in Angola, Ethiopia, Mozambique, and Sudan transformed the drought into a famine that claimed more than one million lives. Bomb damage to relief supply stores of the World Food Program and ICRC compounded the difficulty of delivering food to Afghanistan in late 2001.[117]

Denial of livelihoods

The means to make a living and provide for a family are affected as armed groups target communities for supplies, or prevent people from engaging in commerce. With assets depleted, people are less and less able to cope with external shocks; repeated disruption poses a severe threat to secure supplies of food. Income falls to such a level that people have to reduce the number of meals they eat, and sell their assets to survive.

▶ In Nicaragua, the army distributed AK-47s to coffee farmers for their own protection, but many were stolen and used against the farmers whom they were supposed to protect. Coffee growers in Matagalpa reported a 10.5 per cent rise in production costs in 1999, owing to the additional security measures required to combat this and other armed violence.[119]

▶ In western Tanzania, thieves used arms from refugee camps to rob Lake Victoria fishermen of their fish, money, and nets. Without the means to make a living, the fishermen pour agrochemicals into the lake to kill the fish, which then float to the surface, where they can be collected and sold at local markets. This is causing environmental pollution, health problems, and spiralling poverty among the fishing communities.[120]

Denial of health care

Armed insecurity is a hazard to health. Acute health problems cannot be treated if people are denied access to health services. Gunshot wounds were found to be the leading cause of injuries and deaths from 1994 to 1999 in Gulu, Uganda, yet only 13 per cent of those injured were able to reach a health-care facility within one hour, and only 40 per cent in six hours. The majority of people with severe injuries will not survive if they do not obtain treatment within a couple of hours.[123] Maternal and child mortality – key indicators for the Millennium Development Goals – increase markedly in contexts of armed violence. When 200 troops passed through Boga district of the DRC, staff and two women awaiting caesarian-section operations fled the hospital. Staff later heard that they had both died at home in agonising labour.[124]

The standard of care from health services declines during outbreaks of fighting and conflict. Health facilities are targeted; equipment is destroyed or looted, as in Iraq in early 2003, when hospital ambulances in Mosul were stolen at gunpoint.[125] The number of qualified staff declines as they flee the country, as in Bosnia, or are killed and injured, as in Rwanda. A high incidence of firearm injuries requiring hospital treatment also produces competition for resources. Routine health work suffers as resources are focused on those with more urgent weapons-related injuries and allocated to hospitals nearer the front line,[126] or even to services within the same hospital.[127]

Communicable diseases that can be controlled relatively successfully in peace time become major killers, because vaccination programmes are impossible during armed conflict, and the greater movement of people provides opportunities for infection. Since war broke out in 1998, there has been a sharp increase in diseases such as cholera, measles, polio, plague, and meningitis in the Democratic Republic of Congo. During the conflict in Croatia and Bosnia, rates of tuberculosis increased by half, and outbreaks of hepatitis A were reported in Bosnia.[128]

Denial of education

Conflict and armed crime hamper education. Schools are closed in response to danger, damage, and lack of teachers; sometimes schools are appropriated for other purposes, such as housing for displaced people. In larger Brazilian cities, it is not uncommon for classes to be interrupted or schools closed because of gunfire during territorial battles between rival drug gangs or clashes with police.[129] In Djugu, north-eastern DRC, armed disputes resulted in the destruction of 211 out of a total of 228 educational facilities, and more than 60 per cent of students and teachers

'There are incidents like when the health centre was in the middle of crossfire between gangs. Or like once, when gangs posted snipers in key places who shot at people arriving or leaving the health centres. All this makes our staff afraid; on one occasion the doctor's car was shot at. Another time, the staff had to remain inside due to the shootings outside.'

A health worker in Medellín, Colombia, 2001[122]

withdrew from school.[130] More than half of school-age children in Brazil reported that it was easy to obtain firearms near the school, and of these, about 70 per cent said that guns were used in violent incidents at school.[131]

Development derailed

Weapons in the wrong hands have acute, immediate impacts on personal, economic, social, civil, and political rights, which translate into longer-term effects that prevent development. Development means giving people choices, through building their capacities and creating an environment for them to develop their full potential and lead productive, creative lives; but this cannot happen when people live in fear of the misuse of arms, whether by state or non-state actors. Human development depends on peace and personal security, and thus sustainable development is a victim of insecurity. Poor development indicators go hand in hand with insecurity and conflict.

The Millennium Development Goals[134] grew out of the Millennium Summit in September 2000, when UN member states reaffirmed their commitment to working towards a world in which sustaining development and eliminating poverty would have the highest priority. They focus the efforts of the world community on achieving significant, measurable improvements in people's lives. Yet for countries caught in the cycle of poverty and conflict, they seem completely out of reach.

Countries experiencing civil war 1997-2001

56% of low-development countries

30% of medium-development countries

2% of high-development countries

'Small arms are destroying our lives and livelihoods, and they are serving no good. Poverty levels here are the highest in the country, and the infiltration is worsening our poverty. Without arms we would be very happy – just left with our spears to look after our animals.'

Hassan Odha, Community Development Programme Officer, Northern Kenya, 2002[133]

The development of countries is defined here by the UN Human Development Index which is a composite measure, incorporating indicators relating to income, education, and life expectancy.[135]

A vicious circle

Poverty fuels conflict : As per capita income halves, the risk of civil war roughly doubles.*

Conflict fuels poverty : A typical civil war leaves a country 15% poorer, with around 30% more people living in absolute poverty.**

*Development and Peace, Paul Collier in *Global Future, First Quarter 2003* **The global menace of local strife, *The Economist*, 24 May 2003

Opportunity costs of military spending

While most people would accept that some military spending is inevitable, it must be acknowledged that it competes with many aspects of civilian spending – on infrastructure, education, health care, environmental protection, the police, and so on. In developing economies, defence spending has a negative impact on the rate of economic growth.[137] In more advanced economies, there is no consensus that increased military expenditure is good for the economy;[138] some economists believe that reductions in military spending can improve economic performance, particularly when the savings are reallocated.[139]

After conflict, governments tend to keep military spending high, to guard against future insurgency. Military spending consumes on average 2.8 per cent of governments' budgets before conflict, 5 per cent during conflict, and 4.5 per cent in the first decade of peace after civil war. Yet this expenditure is mortgaging a country's development: research shows that money could often be better spent on health care and education, signalling the government's intentions for peace and encouraging private investment.[140]

While there are, of course, non-economic reasons for defence spending, and real threats that defence expenditure is intended to confront, there are too many cases in which money has been spent neither for legitimate reasons nor for purposes of defence.

▶ South Africa agreed in 1999 to purchase armaments worth US$ 6bn, including frigates, submarines, aircraft, and helicopters. The controversial deal has been the subject of prolonged parliamentary scrutiny and other official inquiries, as well as legal action by a non-government organisation (NGO) to challenge the legality of the deal under the South African constitution.[142] Six billion dollars would purchase treatment with combination therapy for all five million AIDS sufferers for two years.[143]

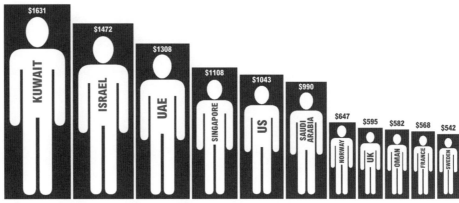

Countries which spent the most on arms per head of population
Source: Data from the *Human Development Report, 2002*.

► Tanzania spent US$ 40m on a joint civil-military air traffic control system in 2001/2. According to experts, this system was overpriced and inappropriate for its use,[144] and an unsuitable use of money in a country in which 46 per cent of the population are undernourished, and where US$ 40m could have provided basic health care for 3.5 million people.

Nearly half of the countries with the highest defence burden have low indicators of human development. Angola and Eritrea spend more than 20 per cent of their gross domestic product (GDP) on the military.[141]

Economic and infrastructural losses

Economic gains are lost as countries seriously affected by armed violence slide into instability. Trade and production are disrupted, tourists stay away, and state management of infrastructure and national resources may be disrupted. A detailed study estimated the cost of the war in Sri Lanka up to 1998 at a staggering US$ 20.8 billion – of which 23 per cent was war-related expenditure, 9 per cent related to damages, and 67 per cent stemmed from loss of output.[146] In Africa, the economic losses due to wars are estimated to be US$ 15 bn per year.[147]

► Armed violence prompts skilled staff and educated people to flee, and financial investment to be withdrawn, depressing economic activity, with particularly onerous impacts upon the landless and urban poor.[148]

► Infrastructure is hard hit. During the 1991 Gulf War, bombs targeted installations used for civilian as well as military purposes, including the electrical supply that was critical for operating Iraq's water and sanitation systems.[149]

► Foreign direct investment is reduced, because violent conflict is not something that most investors are willing to tolerate. In Mozambique, foreign direct investment amounted to US$ 12m per year during the war and US$ 443m per year immediately after it.

► The black market thrives, to the detriment of the national economy. A study links the collapse of the Thai Baht in the late 1990s to inflows of illegal profits from weapons merchants who used the stock and property markets to launder their proceeds.[150]

The excessive diversion of resources – to fund arms purchases and to mitigate the problems caused directly by armed violence – reduces the ability of countries to promote development and achieve the Millennium Development Goals.

Expenditures on health services to deal with the effects of violence amounted to 1.3 per cent of the gross domestic product in Mexico, 1.9 per cent in Brazil, 4.3 per cent in El Salvador, and 5 per cent in Colombia.[145]

Chapter 3
Why act now?

Young boy with toy machine gun picks his way through the rubble of his neighbourhood in Shanghai which is being cleared to make way for modern skyscrapers.

3: Why act now?

The situation is critical.

1. The 'war on terror' has fundamentally shifted some governments' policies. More arms are being exported with little regard for the recipient countries' track record on human rights and humanitarian law, and to countries with whom alliances have been formed purely on the basis of the existence of a common enemy.

2. Civilian casualties are increasingly severe, and modern weapons exacerbate this trend.

3. Weapons possession is becoming more widespread and destructive in many societies.

  ▶ Guns are bound up in notions of masculinity, disadvantaging women, militarising communities, and exacerbating cultures of violence.

  ▶ Violence escalates as more people own guns, and traditional controls break down.

  ▶ The effects of armed organised crime, particularly relating to drugs, are similar to those resulting from war. Children's lives are shattered.

4. The supply of arms is becoming even more out of control – see Chapter Four.

Neither the misuse of arms nor armed conflict is new. In various forms they have both been in existence for millennia, so why the call to action now? The fact is that the global abuse of arms has reached a critical point. Small arms, the 'weapons of mass destruction' that are used every day, are being overlooked. The 'war on terror' has ironically fuelled the proliferation of weapons. In addition, government forces and armed groups who have easy access to weapons and a disregard for human life are increasingly targeting civilians. All this is happening in a context of societal change, where guns play an ever-increasing role in the lives of people in countries around the world.

The 'war on terror'

Most governments have identified international 'terrorism' and weapons of mass destruction as grave threats which must be tackled. These can be effectively addressed only in accordance with international law. The fight against them must not be conducted at the expense of a wider campaign for peace and justice.

At a time when 'fighting terrorism' has been allowed to dominate the international agenda, one would expect that there would be a rekindled interest in arms controls and renewed efforts to prevent arms reaching those who commit abuses. Yet the reverse has occurred.

European countries, and others, claim to base their arms-export criteria on respect for human rights; the USA has a specific law – known as the Leahy Amendments – to ban military aid and training to particular units of foreign security forces that commit human rights abuses.[153] Yet these principles are being swept aside in the fight against 'terrorism'.

The world's most economically powerful states constitute the Group of Eight (G8): Canada, France, Germany, Italy, Japan, the Russian Federation, the UK, and the USA. In June 2002, the G8 allocated US$ 20 billion and agreed a 'global partnership' to prevent terrorists acquiring weapons of mass destruction. But the G8 failed to address the proliferation of conventional weapons, including small arms, to states and armed groups that they know will abuse such weapons to terrorise civilian populations.

Indeed, the UK, USA, France, Germany, Canada, and Italy have approved enormous arms supplies to Saudi Arabia, knowing that the authorities there do not permit any criticism of the state, that all parties or political organisations in Saudi Arabia are illegal, and that thousands of political or religious detainees have been arbitrarily detained over the years.[154]

In the wake of the attacks in the USA on 11 September 2001, the US government has massively increased its military aid to dozens of countries. Some of the recipients of this aid are armed forces which have committed grave violations of human rights and have been identified in the State Department's own human rights report as having a 'poor' human rights record, or worse. Recipient countries include Armenia, Azerbaijan, Afghanistan, Colombia, Georgia, Israel, Nepal, Tajikistan, Turkey, and Yemen. In the cases of Azerbaijan, India, Pakistan, Tajikistan, and Yugoslavia, sanctions were lifted. In some other countries, restrictions had to be relaxed.

'America encourages and expects governments everywhere to help remove the terrorist parasites that threaten their own countries and peace in the world... If governments need training or resources to meet this commitment, America will help.'
US President George W. Bush, 2002[152]

In the year following the 11 September attacks, security assistance and related aid from the USA to Uzbekistan increased by US$ 45 million.[155] In Pakistan, it soared from US$ 3.5 million to US$ 1.3 billion. Meanwhile systematic violations of human rights – including torture, deaths in custody, and extra-judicial killings – by members of the security and paramilitary forces in those countries continue. In March 2002 the US Administration introduced an emergency supplemental defence authorisation bill which sought to lift restrictions on Indonesia and Colombia, despite reports of continuing human rights abuses there.[156]

Stoking the fires of conflict in Colombia

In 2000, the US government approved Plan Colombia: a massive programme of military aid, totalling more than US$ 1.3 bn, most of it destined for the Colombian army, despite the army's poor human rights record and continuing international concern over links between the security forces and paramilitary groups.[158]

Despite a catalogue of evidence that weapons are used for serious human rights violations, the US Administration has extended Colombia's eligibility for military and police training, and gained Congressional support for direct military aid for Colombia's operations against armed rebels, shifting the focus from 'counter-narcotics' to 'counter-terrorism' and enabling the supply of even more weapons.[159]

Close US allies, such as the UK government, appeared to follow suit. The value of British arms cleared for export to Indonesia rose from £2m in 2000 to over £40m in 2002, a 20-fold increase.[157]

The gross abuses of human rights that armed forces allied to the 'war on terror' inflict on civilian populations are given little attention. Arms and military assistance are being offered as a geopolitical inducement, with few, if any, conditions to protect human rights.[160] Indeed, the USA did not investigate or act when its Afghan allies, the Northern Alliance, were implicated in war crimes when their Taliban captives suffocated in sealed transport containers in Kunduz.[161] This sends a message that human rights are secondary in the fight against 'terrorism'. In the case of Uzbekistan, steps were taken to increase the monitoring of human rights, and Congress requires reports of the use to which Uzbek units put US support. However, according to Human Rights Watch, the State Department has since 'exaggerated the human rights gains, in order to maintain foreign assistance', thereby undermining the initiative and reinforcing the message that human rights are negotiable.[162]

Excuses for arms abuses

The unlikely alliances formed by the US government under President George W. Bush have been based on the false logic of 'the enemy of my enemy is my friend'. This crude policy does not begin to take into account the long life-cycles of most weapon systems, and the need for a very careful assessment of the likely ability of armed forces to uphold the rule of law. Yet on this basis, US arms sales to Iraq's neighbours were increased in the build-up to the war in Iraq, and major deals, including some long-stalled, moved forward.[164]

Major arms manufacturing and exporting powers belonging to the G8, as well as China, have played a key role in supplying weapons, directly or indirectly, to regimes which pay only lip service to human rights and international law. Iraq invaded Kuwait in 1990 with weapons bought from all major arms powers.[165] During the Iraq–Iran war in the 1980s, the US government supplied the Iraqis with military intelligence and advice; it also ensured that Iraq had military weaponry, and in one instance it used a Chilean company to supply cluster bombs. Diplomatic relations between Iraq and the USA were reinstated, despite the 'almost daily use of chemical weapons' at that time.[166]

Forging and funding military allegiances purely on the basis of a common enemy and without respect for human rights can result in the opposite of what was intended. Since the 1980s, the US administration has provided vast shipments of arms and military assistance to government and armed opposition groups in Afghanistan, Angola, the Democratic Republic of Congo, Iraq, and Somalia; in all of these countries, armed forces were committing gross violations of human rights while receiving US military aid, and all of them were later accused by US governments of 'harbouring terrorists', or the armed forces concerned were accused by the USA of being 'terrorists'. Years later in Afghanistan and Somalia, the arms received and the techniques learned were used against US armed forces – a phenomenon known as 'blowback'. US forces were attacked with Stinger missile systems in Afghanistan in 2001, which had previously been supplied by the US Central Intelligence Agency to the Afghan Mujahideen forces fighting the Soviet army in the 1980s.[167]

The supply of arms in situations like these stores up problems for the future – creating regional arms races, providing a source of arms for possible diversion to armed groups, and weakening international standards on human rights. The provision of arms must be made dependent on established and unwavering factors, such as strict institutionalised compliance with international human rights and humanitarian law, and it must be separated from short-sighted foreign policy which does not take these longer-term issues into account.

'Fast changes are taking place around the world, especially since September 11, and many countries are reassessing the military balance of powers around them and feel the need to upgrade their systems.'

Major General Avraham Rotem, Israeli defence expert, 2003[163]

The civilian toll keeps rising

The direct and indirect impacts of war and violence have already reached a critical point and will become even more significant over the next 20 years, imposing an intolerable burden on poor communities. By 2020, the numbers of deaths and injuries from war and violence will overtake the numbers of deaths caused by killer diseases such as measles and malaria, without concerted action now to reverse current trends.[169]

Most wars today are fought *within* nations. Conflicts often involve several different armed forces, sometimes divided along ethnic lines. They usually involve irregular forces fighting in civilian areas. The civilian casualty figures show the impact of these trends. Best estimates are that 14 per cent of total casualties were civilians in the First World War. This increased to 67 per cent in the Second World War, and has grown even higher in many of today's wars.[171]

For example, in the Democratic Republic of Congo and in Colombia the distinction between civilians and combatants is often blurred by the actions of government and illegal armed actors alike. Civilians are used as a cover for military and paramilitary operations, as a shield against air or artillery attacks, and as providers of subsistence, shelter, and sexual gratification – mostly at the point of a gun. They are then attacked in reprisal killings and suffer the denial of material aid. Combatants tend to use civilian infrastructure, telecommunications, and logistics for military purposes – making the distinction between military and civilian targets very difficult.

'Conflict diamonds' and arms trafficking to Africa

The diamonds-for-arms trade in Liberia and the Democratic Republic of Congo involves complex networks of aviation businesses, arms merchants, and shipping agents. According to UN investigations in 2000 and 2001, two of the key traffickers were Victor Bout, a Russian businessman then based in the United Arab Emirates, and Sanjivan Ruprah, a Kenyan national based in Liberia.[172] One shipment in November 2000 consisted of Slovakian-made sub-machine guns which were officially destined for Guinea; but the aeroplane transporting them – an Ilyushin controlled by Victor Bout – travelled instead to Liberia.[173] On its way back, the plane stopped over in Kisangani, where Sanjivan Ruprah had been granted a 4,000 km^2 diamond concession by the DRC authorities.[174] The plane also picked up sub-machine guns in Uganda destined for Liberia in a deal involving Sanjivan Ruprah.[175] He has attempted to sell his diamonds in Belgium, where he was arrested in February 2002 by the Belgian authorities for counterfeiting and using a false passport.[176]

Deadly privatisation of conflict

In civil wars, the forces involved are increasingly turning to plunder of natural resources and extortion from civilians to fund the conflict or, indeed, as a primary purpose for the continuation of conflict. Armed forces feed off civilians, using terrible violence and threats, forcing communities to provide shelter, food, money, recruits, and sexual services.

Diamonds in Angola and Sierra Leone; oil in Sudan and Angola; copper in Papua New Guinea; timber in Cambodia and Liberia; coltan, gold, and other minerals in the Democratic Republic of Congo: these resources are exploited and traded by governments and local military commanders in exchange for military supplies and personal financial gain. A desperate government will sometimes mortgage its country's future stores of precious natural resources in order to raise immediate finance to obtain weapons and ammunition. In Rwanda before the genocide, the tea plantations were mortgaged for the purchase of arms from Egypt.[178] In the Republic of Congo, prior to the massacres in Brazzaville in 1997, future oil production was sold to obtain arms.[179]

In about a quarter of the over 40 armed conflicts around the world in 2001, control of natural resources played a significant role, generating at least US\$ 12 bn a year.[180] In these situations, economic power and armed power go hand in hand, with one reinforcing the other, leaving those in control of the exploitation largely above the law.

Reports by the UN Panel of Experts on Liberia, which monitors compliance with the UN arms embargo, have identified the role of timber exports in funding this tragic war, in which both sides have abused the human rights of civilians. In addition, timber companies are reported to have facilitated transfers of weapons.[181]

In many of these wars, the capacity to influence belligerents is severely limited. As they develop independent means of financing, and break free from the foreign ideological control that characterised the Cold War era, they care less what outsiders think or say, and feel free to commit grave breaches of international human rights and humanitarian law with impunity. Cutting the source of the weaponry and/or ending the trade in resources is one of the only ways to influence their behaviour.

'Our diamonds are being exchanged for guns, and they are coming in through the back way. If I had the power, no one would ever trade in arms in my country, because I have seen war. I appeal to the people who sell arms to our brothers to destroy us, to stop doing it.'

Chief Mohammed Koroma, Boajibu, Sierra Leone, 2001[177]

Private military companies

Private military companies contracted to undertake direct military services on behalf of governments or opposition forces play a critical and increasing role in the provision of arms and support to regimes around the world. Private companies are often ideally placed to import weapons, with links to governments, arms brokers, air cargo companies, and arms manufacturers. One company supplied weapons to both sides in the Sierra Leone conflict.[182] The number and influence of private companies are increasing, and many believe that the 'war on terror' will only accelerate this trend. In recent years, the US government has frequently hired or authorised private military consultants to train foreign police forces and military troops. According to a detailed study, US companies trained military forces in more than 24 countries during the 1990s, including Angola, Bolivia, Bosnia, Colombia, Croatia, Egypt, Equatorial Guinea, Ethiopia, Haiti, Kosovo, Liberia, Nigeria, Peru, Rwanda, and Saudi Arabia.[183] The US government has not taken adequate steps to ensure that where such training is given, especially in the use of arms, the training courses promote strict adherence to international human rights and humanitarian law.[184]

Guns in society – spiralling out of control

The culture of armed violence is becoming all-pervasive in peace time as well as at times of conflict. It is a matter of debate to decide which came first, the gun or the culture of violence, but it is clear that they are mutually reinforcing. In cultures where carrying weapons is traditional, men have replaced traditional weapons, such as bows and arrows, with guns; men in other cultures are newly adopting weapons. In both cases there is a prospect of an alarming escalation of violence. Can men live without the gun? Do they want to?

Men, women, and guns

The power of guns is inextricably linked with the notion of masculinity in both industrialised and traditional cultures. Most weapons are owned and used by men; in the USA only nine per cent of women own guns, as opposed to 42 per cent of men, while in Canada 85 per cent of gun owners are men.[186] Most armed forces do not include women (although the Eritrean army and the Tamil Tigers are renowned for their recruitment of women), and often women are excluded from firearms duties in the security services.

'We do not have any toys to play with... so we make a gun out of some sticks... and that is how we play. I can dismantle my father's T56. Sometimes my father tells me to clean his gun. Now I am quite skilled at dismantling and re-assembling the gun... My main ambition is to join the army...'

Sri Lankan child, 1998[185]

Conventional notions of masculinity ascribe the role of protector and defender to men, and in many cultures this role has become symbolised by the possession of a gun. Gun ownership has become a symbol of masculine power and status, with a hint of glamour, attractive to both women and men. For example, in Brazil the expression 'Maria AK-47' is commonly used to describe women who are attracted to men because of the guns they carry, in a twist to the expression 'Maria gasoline', which refers to women who choose men based on their cars.[188]

In traditionally armed cultures – including, for example, areas of Albania, Afghanistan, Uganda, and Somalia – the gun becomes an extension of the male self. Kalashnikovs are to Yemeni tribesmen 'what baseball caps are to Americans'.[189]

Guns may become an integral part of boys' lives in such cultures:

▶ At the birth of a boy, guns are fired joyfully into the air, and people exclaim, 'We have increased by one gun!'[190]

▶ When a boy receives his first gun, he becomes a man: at the Acholi coming-of-age ceremony in Uganda, ashes are rubbed on the boy's body, and everyone blesses the gun.[191]

▶ Boys have been dropping out of school in northern Kenya to become *moran* (warriors).[192]

▶ In Somalia, arms are so central that parents have named male infants 'Uzi' or 'AK'.[193]

Where guns are perceived as glamorous and exciting and bestow high status upon the bearer, it is not surprising that children absorb this. According to a former youth worker in north London, *'Children come out of school talking about guns. The mentality is so much more vicious now. They don't talk about beating each other up. They talk about killing each other. The simple fact is that with a gun, you are someone, you can hold your own. Without one, you are a dead man.'*

The power of guns is both symbolic and actual: they need not always be used to have impact. The ownership and use of arms reinforce existing gender inequalities, strengthening the dominant position of men, maintaining women's subordination through violence and the threat of violence. Women can be perceived as objects, attainable to those with guns, because guns bestow power, and power grants access to the most beautiful women, also symbols of power.[194]

Male violence against women and girls is often reinforced by cultures of weaponry: guns become an extension of male physical power, facilitating and exacerbating domestic and sexual violence, and coercion. Violent disputes in the home often become more lethal to women and girls when men have guns.

'The men who shot these girls consider themselves outside the law. They carry guns as male jewellery – to be 'gangstas' – and eventually they will use them. Unless we find a way to make them feel included, they will continue to kill and maim – because they have no value system other than brand names.'

University worker in Birmingham, UK, after the killing of two girls, January 2003[187]

While boys interviewed in South Africa felt that girls prefer men who have guns, girls in the same community said that boys used guns to coerce them into sexual relations.[195]

Reducing the influence and availability of weapons is one key factor in tackling domestic violence and ensuring women's fundamental right to personal security.

Kids using guns

Children[198] belonging to armed gangs and combat forces have their childhoods destroyed; they are often traumatised, unprepared and unsuited for a 'normal' life. Once they grow up, finding a job, forming a family, and finding a stable place in society can be extremely difficult. Young people are particularly vulnerable, because they may have known no other way of life than a gun culture; they have no other social construct as a frame of reference and hence can less easily avoid being absorbed into it. They find themselves alienated from society, ill-equipped to restart their lives, but they can always resort to the way of life that they know best – violence.

One of the reasons why so many children are involved in armed conflict and armed crime is the simplicity and ease of use of small arms and light weapons: semi-automatic rifles are now light enough and simple enough to be stripped, reassembled, and used by a child of 10.

▶ It is estimated that 300,000 children are working as soldiers in conflicts all around the world, in official armed forces and armed opposition groups, with the highest numbers in Africa and Asia. Myanmar (Burma) is believed to have the largest number of child soldiers in the world, with as many as 70,000 boys serving in the national army.[199]

▶ Many thousands more belong to criminal armed gangs, where conditions can be surprisingly similar. According to some estimates, at least 25,000 children belong to gangs in El Salvador,[200] and between 5,000 and 6,000 children carry weapons in Rio city, Brazil, alone.[201] According to the PanAmerican Health Organisation, only 25 per cent of children in gangs have completed elementary school.[202]

Weapons in more hands

Gun ownership and the culture of violence is significant in post-conflict societies where violence has become legitimised, and in urban settings where more and more criminals, gangs, and private security forces are armed, increasing the pressure on private individuals to acquire arms for their own protection. The media must share some of the responsibility: both for glorifying guns and sometimes for exaggerating the dangers and exacerbating fear.[205]

Civilian ownership of arms, legal or illegal under national laws, is rising in many places, with China and South Asia becoming major centres of arms ownership.[206] Some countries, such as the UK and Australia, have tightened their gun laws after specific incidents of gun-related violence, but increased incidents of armed crime suggest that illegal ownership has been little affected.

Guns can become so central to communities that their role goes far beyond their original purpose. In South Africa, AK-47s were used as currency and described as 'Soweto Black Cheques'; in Georgia, arms were a more stable medium of exchange than roubles in the early 1990s: one English teacher was paid in grenades for lessons provided to an elderly woman.[207]

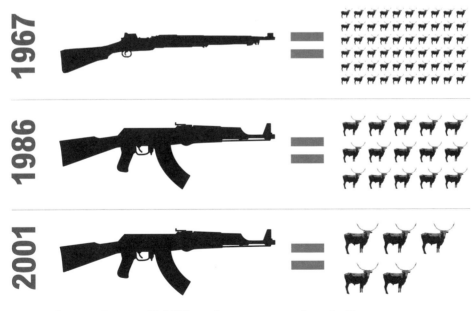

Increasing availability reduces arms prices in Kenya
According to Joshua Katta, a Pokot chief in Kolowa, Kenya.
Source: Karl Vick, 'Small arms global reach uproots tribal traditions', *Washington Post*, 8 July 2001.

Guns in official hands are easily outnumbered by those in civilian possession.[203]

'In my village, every man has a gun, a gun of his own. Now, if you don't have one for yourself then, "Yu nogat nem" – you don't have a name in the village. Your wife can be raped. They can steal. They can do anything to you.'
Francis Danga, Papua New Guinea, 2000[204]

'Give everything to your friend, except your car, your wife, and your gun.'
Iraqi saying, reported by journalists in Iraq, 2003[208]

Escalating violence in pastoralist areas

Fundamental changes in the traditional way of life in pastoralist communities[210] in East Africa are occurring because of the easy availability of weapons. Livestock rustling is part of this culture, but there are rules: for example, the raiders announce their presence by drums and chants, never by ambush, and allow surrendering men to run away; women and children were always spared. However, now that large numbers of weapons are available, these traditions are being lost.

In one instance in northern Kenya a few years ago, young Pokot tribesmen brandishing AK-47s raided their neighbours, the Marakwet. Forty-seven people were killed, most of whom were women and children;[211] schools, houses, and shops were burned to the ground. Such brutality and destruction were previously unheard of.

Power and authority used to rest with the village elders, but the latter are now deferring to those who carry guns. Among the once peaceful Marakwet, many have adopted the Pokot custom of wearing bead necklaces to glorify violence: white beads mean that the wearer has taken a life. And certainly no one is talking about giving up weapons since this raid.[212]

Guns, crime, and the lethal drugs link

Armed criminality is increasing in many countries in the world. In the UK, firearm use increased by 35 per cent in 2002;[213] firearms-related homicides are uncommon, but have gone up over the last few years, especially in big cities.[214] Three quarters of the firearms seized by police in London were air pistols, converted by gangs into .22 mm and .38 mm cartridge pistols, and supplied by one UK company from stock made in Germany.[215] In South Africa, illegal weapons ownership is increasing, all types of crime involving firearms have increased, and firearms-related homicide as a proportion of total homicides is increasing annually, from 41 per cent in 1994 to 49.3 per cent in 2000.[216] In the USA, armed homicides have been declining from a peak in 1993, but the tide may be turning again, and gang activity and gun violence are re-emerging in some cities.[217]

Violence is escalating as criminals acquire more lethal weapons. In the Netherlands, incidents involving firearms increased from 8 to 15 per day from 1994 to 1999, and criminals are replacing their handguns with more powerful weapons, such as machine guns.[218] In Central America, armed crime and violence is increasing, with criminals using military-style weapons left over from previous civil wars.[219]

Nearly eight million small arms are newly manufactured every year, the majority going into civilian hands – like a tap open on full, pouring out new weapons to add to the global pool.[220]

In cases of extreme urban violence, as in parts of Brazil and elsewhere, fighting among territorial factions and with police has escalated to such a point that deaths and injuries are comparable – or worse – to situations where war has been officially declared.[222]

Illegal drugs militarise communities. The cultivation, processing, and distribution of drugs establish and concentrate power in the hands of those involved; they create an environment dominated by guns, used to protect and maintain the powerful interests involved, to stifle dissent, and to extort 'taxation'. This is true both in the rural areas where farmers cultivate the plants, often under extreme economic pressure, and also in urban areas of both developed and developing countries, where drug dealers rule swathes of cities. A huge increase in firearms homicides was seen in parts of the USA and Brazil in the early 1990s, reflecting the rise in gang wars over the trade in crack cocaine.[223]

Armed groups are often intimately linked with drugs trafficking. An estimated 95 per cent of the world's opium comes from war-torn nations;[224] drugs bankroll armed groups in Afghanistan and Myanmar (Burma), to name just two countries. Arms and drugs often travel on the same routes in different directions, using the same operators, middle-men, and carriers. Revenues from drugs finance the purchase of arms, ammunition, military equipment, uniforms, and other items; sometimes weapons are bartered directly. The Golden Triangle, a border area between Thailand, Myanmar (Burma), and Laos known for the production of opium and methamphetamine ('speed'), has earned a new reputation as a haven through which regional rebel groups traffic AK-47 and M-16 assault rifles, rocket-propelled grenades, landmines, and even surface-to-air missiles.[225]

There are incidences of law-enforcement agencies misusing arms in attempts to tackle illegal drug trafficking. In February 2003, the Prime Minister of Thailand announced a 'war on drugs'. The effect of the government's campaign against drug trafficking has been criticised as a *de facto* policy of shooting to kill anyone believed to be involved in the drugs trade.[226] Three weeks later, Amnesty International expressed grave concern about hundreds of reported killings of drug-trafficking suspects by the Thai security forces: *'It is a sad fact that after 10 years of significant improvement in Thailand's human rights record, the government has now taken a big step backwards.'*

'Narcotics are going north, but illegal arms and ammunition are coming south.'

Ronald Gajraj, Guyana's Minister of Home Affairs, 2002[221]

'I'm afraid. But the object is to make the other gang member fear me more. If I'm strapped, [wearing a weapon] then I'm even.'

Gang member in California, USA, 2003[227]

Chapter 4
The arms bazaar

Guns for sale. A man window shopping for firearms in Darra bazaar, Pakistan.

4: The arms bazaar

'My point of view is that these manufacturers should be stopped. The world powers, Britain, France, the USA, and so on could help. Guns are not made for animals in the bush. Rocket launchers are not made for animals in the bush...You are making them to kill who? To kill me and you!'

Peter Rashid, Boajibu, Sierra Leone, 2001[228]

The lack of arms controls allows some to profit from the misery of others.

▶ While international attention is focused on the need to control weapons of mass destruction, the trade in conventional weapons continues to operate in a legal and moral vacuum.

▶ More and more countries are starting to produce small arms, many with little ability or will to regulate their use.

▶ Permanent UN Security Council members – the USA, UK, France, Russia, and China - dominate the world trade in arms.

▶ Most national arms controls are riddled with loopholes or barely enforced.

▶ Key weaknesses are lax controls on the brokering, licensed production, and 'end use' of arms.

▶ Arms get into the wrong hands through weak controls on firearm ownership, weapons management, and misuse by authorised users of weapons.

From 1998 to 2001, the USA, the UK, and France earned more income from arms sales to developing countries than they gave in aid.[229]

While the world's attention is focused on the need to control weapons of mass destruction, the trade in conventional weapons continues unabated, with no global control. Both the state-sanctioned trade and the illicit trade in arms must be tackled, in order to prevent irresponsible use of arms and the horrific human cost that ensues.

A unique industry

The monetary value of international authorised exports of arms is relatively small in global terms, amounting to around US$ 21 billion per year – representing half of one per cent of total world trade, and less than half of the value of the global coffee market. Yet these statistics completely belie the international significance of the arms trade. First, unlike other industries, many of the products manufactured and sold are specifically designed to kill and injure human beings. Second, the permanent members of the UN Security Council – China, France, the Russian Federation, the UK, and the USA – are firmly entrenched in this business and profiting from it. In terms of financial value of conventional arms sales, in 2001 (the most recent year for which figures are available) they were the top five arms exporters in the world, together responsible for 88 per cent of conventional arms exports. The USA dominates the industry, contributing almost half (45 per cent) of all the world's exported weapons.[231]

'A gun is as easy to get as a pack of cigarettes.'

Evan Jean Lolless, aged 34, serving life imprisonment for murder in the USA, 1997[230]

Big industry operates in a global control vacuum

There are many ways in which the arms industry differs from others. According to Transparency International, the arms industry is the second most likely to involve bribes: a report from the US Department of Commerce claimed that the defence sector accounted for 50 per cent of all bribery allegations, even though it constitutes less than one per cent of all trade. Widespread corruption and questionable business practice are perhaps a result of the secrecy surrounding transactions, the complexity of contracts, and the fact that the industry is dominated by a small number of big deals.[232] In addition, the industry often receives a much higher level of official subsidy, with governments actively promoting defence sales in a way unheard of in other sectors: high-ranking government ministers often lobby potential importers directly.

Arms exports and jobs

Many arms-exporting governments – including the UK[233] – often cite the importance of the defence industry to the national economy, with a clear implication that restricting arms exports through a responsible arms-export policy would be economically damaging. However, recent research from the UK suggests that this is far from the case.[234]

▶ A 2001 study, involving Ministry of Defence economists, suggests that a 50 per cent reduction in arms exports by value would lead to modest one-off adjustment costs to the UK economy of around £2bn – £2.5bn. There would be an initial loss of some 49,000 jobs, but as the economy adjusted, around 67,000 new jobs would be created.[235]

▶ Research in 2002 suggests that a responsible arms export policy would necessitate a 27.5 per cent reduction in arms-exports by value, which would entail one-off adjustment costs of £1.1bn – £1.4bn, with an initial loss of 27,000 jobs offset by the eventual creation of 37,000 new jobs.[236]

Both studies clearly show that the financial impact of a responsible arms export policy is relatively modest, and while some jobs will be initially lost in the defence industry, more jobs will be created elsewhere in the longer-term.

The arms industry manufactures products and provides services which maim and kill. One would expect, therefore, a strong degree of control commensurate with this responsibility - governments and industry working together to ensure that these weapons are used and sold responsibly. Yet the arms trade is like no other, operating outside the jurisdiction of the World Trade Organization, the parameters of the UN

Conference on Trade and Development (UNCTAD), and the bounds of the arms non-proliferation regime. The control is left to individual governments, which may be unwilling or unable to ensure responsible practices.

Arming the Philippines

In late 2001, the USA offered the government of the Philippines military equipment worth more than US$ 100 million – including helicopters and transport planes and 30,000 M-16 rifles – to fight various armed groups. The transfers were agreed as part of the US government's 'war on terror'. The US military has also provided counter-insurgency training. This training does not incorporate rigorous human rights safeguards, and systems of military accountability in the Philippines have proved weak. As a result, US military aid risks exacerbating patterns of human rights violations, aggravating local tensions, and prolonging the armed conflict in central Mindanao.[237]

There is already a thriving illegal market in small arms in the Philippines, and there are fears that the injection of military equipment from the USA – which includes small arms – may contribute to a further proliferation of these weapons. Through loss, theft, or illegal sale, munitions originating with the Philippine government forces sometimes end up in the hands of criminal and armed political groups. In Mindanao, for example, more than 70 per cent of the population own one or more guns. Machine-guns can be bought for as little as US$ 375, and revolvers for a mere US$ 15. As many as 82 per cent of homicides involve small arms.[238]

Increasing unregulated production

The Russian Federation has a large defence industry with centralised systems which should mean that exports can be relatively well controlled – yet there are no national legal criteria to ensure that weapons are not exported to destinations where they may be used for violations of international human rights and humanitarian law.[239] In less well regulated economies, such as those of the many developing countries which produce arms, output is usually subject to even less stringent control.

Recent research has identified 1,135 companies manufacturing small arms and ammunition in at least 98 countries; these numbers are increasing all the time.[240] Between 1960 and 1999, the number of countries producing small arms doubled, and there was an almost six-fold increase in the number of companies manufacturing them. While some of this increase can be explained by the privatisation of state industries, the creation of more nation states, and better reporting in the 1990s, the profusion of arms-producing companies and nations presents a clear challenge to those who advocate strong controls.

'Craft' production uncontrolled

At the other end of the scale, domestic or 'craft' production of weapons is widespread in both developed and developing countries. Although the output is much smaller than that of official production, the impact in certain locations is highly significant.

Some of the weapons produced in this way are fairly basic: for example, pipe bombs in Northern Ireland, makeshift pistols made from bedsprings and metal tubing in Honduras and India,[242] and grenades fired from home-made tubes cut from oil pipelines in Colombia.[243] Other weapons are much more sophisticated, and sometimes of surprisingly high quality. The Palestinian group Hamas produces an anti-tank weapon called the 'Al Bana': a 95 mm rocket with a TNT warhead, fired from a plastic pipe one metre in length.[244] In Colombia, the market is overloaded with *hechizas* (home-made weapons) of high quality at competitive prices, produced mainly in Cali and Pereira, and priced at approximately one third of the black-market original: a Walter PPK pistol might cost US$ 350 on the black market, but a home-made copy would cost only US$ 100.[245] Most craft production involves guns, but rebel groups in Sri Lanka and Colombia have improvised tanks built from farm tractors or bulldozers, with cabs protected by armour plate and machine-guns mounted on top.[246]

Uncontrolled arms proliferation

The absence of controls, together with the presence of loopholes or poor enforcement of controls, means that arms travel too easily around the world, reaching conflict zones and countries with poor human rights records or high levels of organised crime. The majority of weapons used in such situations are not home-produced. Arms, particularly small arms, do not respect national borders. One of the key features of the trade in arms is the way that weapons pass from the state-sanctioned sector to the illegal sphere. The boundary between the two is extremely weak and porous.

'We are three brothers who work together. We inherited our business from our father, who inherited it from his. Our grandfather was known in the whole region for his inspired manufacture of hunting rifles... With 31 children between us, it takes 17 kg of rice per day to feed the whole family. So we will not give up our trade for anything in the world.'

Mr Dante, illegal producer of arms in Bamako, Mali, 2003[241]

In Ghana, it takes six months to grow corn or cassava, but only between one and five days to make a gun.[247]

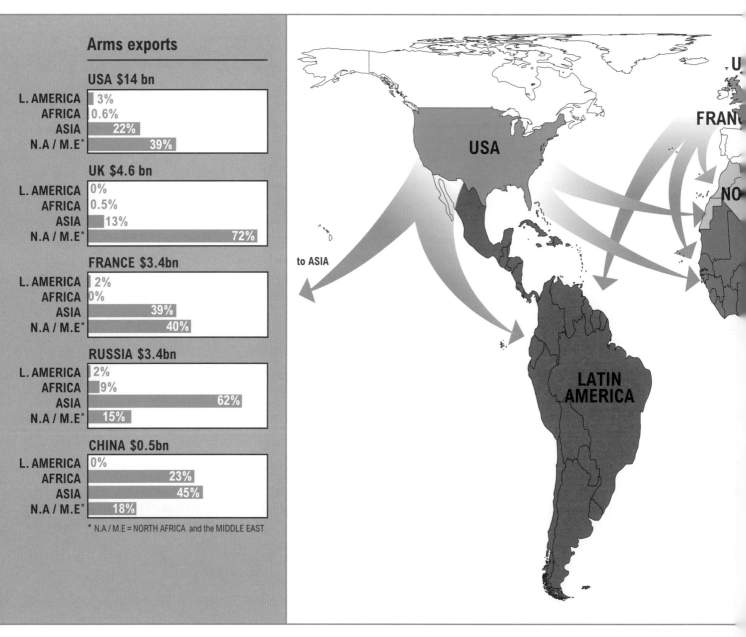

Arms exports

USA $14 bn

L. AMERICA	3%
AFRICA	0.6%
ASIA	22%
N.A / M.E*	39%

UK $4.6 bn

L. AMERICA	0%
AFRICA	0.5%
ASIA	13%
N.A / M.E*	72%

FRANCE $3.4bn

L. AMERICA	2%
AFRICA	0%
ASIA	39%
N.A / M.E*	40%

RUSSIA $3.4bn

L. AMERICA	2%
AFRICA	9%
ASIA	62%
N.A / M.E*	15%

CHINA $0.5bn

L. AMERICA	0%
AFRICA	23%
ASIA	45%
N.A / M.E*	18%

* N.A / M.E = NORTH AFRICA and the MIDDLE EAST

USA

to ASIA

LATIN
AMERICA

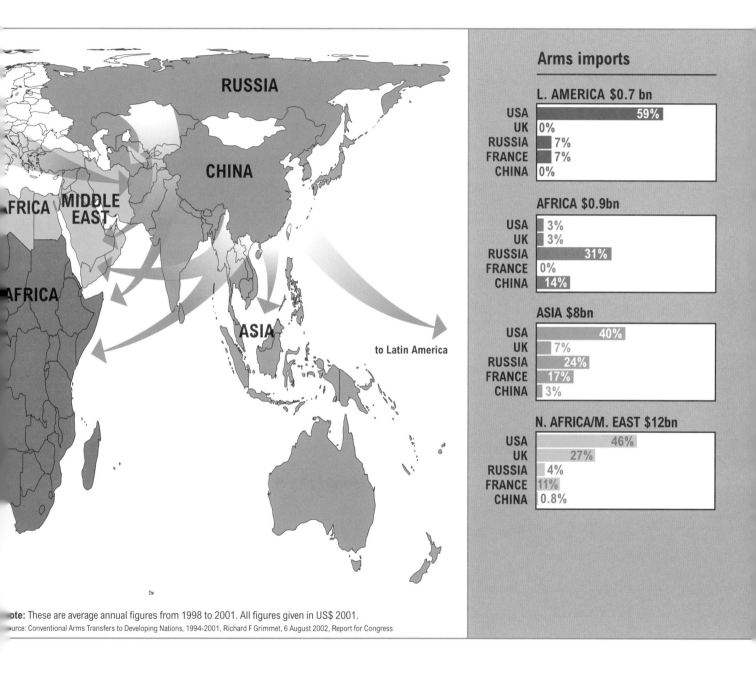

RUSSIA

CHINA

AFRICA

MIDDLE
EAST

AFRICA

ASIA

to Latin America

Arms imports

L. AMERICA $0.7 bn
USA	59%
UK	0%
RUSSIA	7%
FRANCE	7%
CHINA	0%

AFRICA $0.9bn
USA	3%
UK	3%
RUSSIA	31%
FRANCE	0%
CHINA	14%

ASIA $8bn
USA	40%
UK	7%
RUSSIA	24%
FRANCE	17%
CHINA	3%

N. AFRICA/M. EAST $12bn
USA	46%
UK	27%
RUSSIA	4%
FRANCE	11%
CHINA	0.8%

ote: These are average annual figures from 1998 to 2001. All figures given in US$ 2001.

ource: Conventional Arms Transfers to Developing Nations, 1994-2001, Richard F Grimmet, 6 August 2002, Report for Congress

Weaknesses in national arms controls

National governments enact and enforce legislation to control the production, export, national sales, management, and use of arms. Too often these are woefully weak, riddled with loopholes, characterised by wide gaps between policy and practice – and as a result they allow easy access to lethal weaponry.

Arms transfers

'Local, regional and world leaders must accept the fact that we cannot let the free market rule the international arms trade. We must not enrich ourselves through the commerce of death. Rather, we must realise that the arms trade is most often a friend of dictators and an enemy of the people. The time has come to choose human lives over arms.'

Dr Oscar Arias, Nobel Peace Laureate [249]

Because of links with national security and foreign policy, there is a broad international consensus that the export and import of arms should always be subject to authorisation by governments. Yet lack of proper controls means that diversion of arms from the state-sanctioned sector to the illicit sphere is very common. In addition, a government authorisation for sale may be influenced more by the economic or geopolitical importance of the deal than by any concerns over the subsequent impact of the arms, as the following examples show.

▶ As the Soviet Union fragmented, newly created states inherited arms-production facilities at a time when the need for foreign exchange and employment was a national priority over concerns over the use to which the arms would be put.

▶ More recently, in order for India to reach its goal of becoming a net exporter of arms, the government has chosen to abandon its arms-export blacklist.[251]

▶ The Czech Republic, Slovakia, Bulgaria, Romania, and Poland, all modernising their systems and resources in preparation for NATO membership, are dumping old Cold War tanks and heavy artillery on to the military market, making more weapons available for areas of violent conflict.[252]

Responsible governments demand to see an **end-use certificate**, identifying the recipient of exported arms, and the purpose for which they are bought. In practice, diversion is common, because the system is easy to circumvent – either because of complacency on the part of the licensing body, or because of devious or corrupt practices in the production of the certificate. For example:

'We cannot have it both ways. We can't be both the world's leading champion of peace and the world's leading supplier of arms.'

Former US President Jimmy Carter, presidential campaign, 1976 [250]

▶ Canadian government policy banned sales of arms to the Colombian military, on account of the risk that they might be used to violate human rights. However, a loophole in the law allowed 33 Canadian military helicopters to be sent to Colombia via the USA between 1998 and 2000. Canada does not require an end-use certificate for exports to the USA, and the USA provides no re-export guarantees.[253]

Status of international arms controls

Conventional weapons, and particularly small arms, kill more civilians than any other type of weapon, including weapons of mass destruction, so you would expect some tight international controls on their proliferation.

BUT arms-proliferation controls concentrate on weapons of mass destruction; there are almost no binding regulations which relate to the transfer of conventional weapons.

Almost all arms are manufactured legitimately, and only later get transferred into the illicit market, so you would expect strong international controls on the state-sanctioned trade in weapons.

BUT many of the controls on conventional weapons that do exist focus on illicit transfers.

There are some legally binding global controls on the trade in conventional weapons, but not many.

► International arms embargoes are useful mechanisms for limiting the influx of weapons into an area of conflict, but they are reactive rather than preventative, and subject to political influences.
► There are a small number of restrictions on specific weapons which cause indiscriminate suffering, such as landmines.[255]

And there are only a few international agreements to control the export of heavy weapons like tanks and aircraft.

There are no global treaties, and the only regional instrument is in Europe, which has a politically binding Code of Conduct applying to state-sanctioned exports of all arms, as well as several other instruments.[256]

As small arms kill the greatest number of civilians, some controls on these weapons would be expected.

In response to growing concern, a UN process to consider the problem of small arms has begun, and several regional instruments have been created:
► The UN Firearms Protocol tackles illicit manufacture and trafficking of firearms to organised crime; it has been agreed but has not yet come into force.
► Several regions have initiated activities and/or controls to prevent arms proliferation, notably in Africa and the Americas – see Chapter 5.
The regional small-arms programmes have been disappointing, due in part to the absence of provisions relating to international human rights and humanitarian law. Nevertheless, there is no doubt that a new global discussion has begun.
In addition, civil-society organisations working to stop the proliferation and misuse of small arms have joined together in IANSA – the International Action Network on Small Arms – to work together for greater progress and more radical change.

'The ease with which potential adversaries can acquire advanced conventional weapons will present us with new challenges in conventional war.'

Donald Rumsfeld, US Defence Secretary, June 2001[254]

▶ Despite assurances from Israel that 'no UK-originated equipment are [sic] used as part of the defence force's activities in the Territories', modified British Centurion tanks were used by Israeli troops in the West Bank and Gaza in 2002.[259]

Arms **brokering**, via third countries, is a key way by which arms get into the wrong hands. Brokers, supported by transporters and financiers, are middlemen who arrange transfers between sellers and buyers. Arms brokers, transporters, and financiers have been implicated in supplying weapons to the world's worst-affected conflict zones and human rights crisis zones, including those subject to embargoes by the UN – Afghanistan, Angola, DRC, Iraq, Rwanda, Sierra Leone, and South Africa, to name but a few.

Most national arms-export legislation does not fully address the problem of international arms brokering, transporting, or financing; where legislation is in force, unscrupulous brokers may simply move 'off shore' to another country with weaker controls. Electronic banking and tax havens have made international movements of finance much easier to organise and more difficult to trace. Transporters avoid detection by flying planes on circuitous routes, via a number of airports, at night or at low altitudes to avoid radar; sometimes registration numbers are changed, and 'flags of convenience' are used.[260]

Arms technology is exported when an arms company permits the production of its weapons in another country, **under licence**. The establishment of licensed production agreements in countries with a record of internal repression and human rights violations, or countries engaged in conflict, effectively circumvents export-control legislation that would not allow a direct transfer to that country. Often, the original manufacturer has little control once the agreement has been reached: the Bulgaria Arsenal plant continued to produce Kalashnikov rifles 14 years after its licensed production agreement had expired.[261]

Small quantities of arms smuggled over borders by individuals (engaged in what is known as the '**ant trade**') are often purchased lawfully and passed on to others. This occurs in Paraguay, where a tourist can, perfectly legally, buy two guns, providing opportunities for significant inflows of arms to neighbouring countries.[262]

Arms are **recycled** from one conflict to another, and from states with lax controls on civilian ownership. In late 2002, large stocks of surplus ammunition were flown from Albania – after an arms and ammunition collection exercise – to Rwanda, allegedly for use in eastern DRC.[263] Countries torn apart by war, such as Afghanistan, Somalia, Angola and Albania, can be an easy source of illegal weapons.

Arms brokering: a typical illicit arms deal involving several countries[265]

Arms brokers in Guatemala and Panama organised a shipment of 3,117 AK-47 assault rifles and 2.5 million rounds of ammunition to an illegal armed group in Colombia, bought from Nicaraguan police. The brokers claimed to be buying the weapons for police in Panama.

The deal was brokered by two Israeli nationals, claiming to be official representatives of the Israeli government arms industry in Guatemala, and a Panama-based Israeli businessman. Nicaraguan officials did not check with Panama's government to verify the end use of the weapons; Panama claims to know nothing about the deal. It was later found that the government purchase-order used to acquire the arms was actually a skilful forgery.

To avoid detection, the Panamanian ship picked up the AK-47s at the Nicaraguan port of El Bluff, a small dock on the Atlantic coast which is seldom used by anyone but fishermen. The weapons were named in the ship's manifest as children's plastic balls. The ship bypassed Panama, and landed at the remote northern Colombian port of Turbo. Lorries collected the 14 containers and disappeared into the thick jungles of Urabá.

'Mostly the stuff we carried were brand new AKs [Kalashnikov assault rifles] plus the ammunition. It is quite a standard operation for us. ...We know there is a war on. We are not involved in it, because we're just charter pilots really. ...To me it is all freight. But, er, obviously this, er, some of it is not too good.'

Captain Brian 'Sport' Martin, who flew arms from Rwanda and Uganda into the rebel-held town of Kisangani in the Democratic Republic of Congo, 2000[264]

One of the major causes of the increasing availability of small arms in the world markets during the 1990s was the indiscriminate off-loading of standard weapons from members of the former Warsaw Pact to poorer countries.[266] Sometimes, this trend was accelerated by conversion to NATO standard weaponry.[267]

When challenged on their failure to prevent irresponsible arms transfers, some governments have openly employed the morally flawed argument: 'If we don't sell them, someone else will'. When Tony Blair, UK Prime Minister, was asked why the UK was selling British parts for F16 aircraft for onward sale to Israel, when there had been clear evidence that these weapons were being used directly against civilians, he replied: 'What would actually happen if we [refused to sell parts] is not that the parts wouldn't be supplied, is that you would find every other defence industry in the world rushing in to take the place that we have vacated'.[268] Even if this were true, it would not be morally right: it is never right or good policy to sell arms to those who use them to commit atrocities. The USA and the UK, among others, armed Iraq in the 1980s when there was clear evidence that the Iraqi government was guilty of violating the human rights of its own citizens. Why are these lessons from the past not being learned?

Licensed production: circumventing export legislation

Companies in at least 15 countries (Austria, Belgium, the Czech Republic, France, Germany, Israel, Italy, Portugal, Russia, South Africa, Singapore, Sweden, Switzerland, the UK, and the USA) have established agreements to permit the production of small arms and ammunition under licence in 45 other countries.[269] This diffusion of production around the world, often in countries with weak arms-export controls, greatly increases the risks of arms falling into the hands of abusers. For example, Otokar in Turkey produce vehicles which share 70 per cent of the components of UK Land Rovers. The UK government classifies the exports of the components as 'civilian', yet with some modifications they become armoured patrol vehicles and have been sold in Algeria and Pakistan.[270]

Often, powerful governments which profess to respect human rights and offer aid programmes to poor countries also authorise arms supplies which undermine the rule of law. For example, the UK is a key supplier of handguns to the Jamaican police force, which has one of the highest rates of police killings per capita in the world: 600 improperly investigated deaths since 1999. Small arms from Italy have been supplied to police and security forces in Algeria, Democratic Republic of Congo, Kenya, Nigeria, Sierra Leone, and Turkey, despite clear evidence of arms being used for excessive force, torture, and violations of human rights.[271]

It is not arms production *per se* that is questionable, but the sale to irresponsible users, and the absence of controls to prevent arms reaching irresponsible users. The human cost of such sales is clear. Do arms producers really want the blood of civilians on their hands?

Other national controls

The national rules on **firearm ownership** for individuals vary widely from country to country, ranging from no control at all to a complete ban. Even the USA, the most heavily armed nation in the world, has many national and state laws to control the misuse of guns: for example, civilians are not allowed to buy military assault rifles.[272] Yet such restrictions are often seriously inadequate: they contain significant loopholes, or they are not enforced. In Colombia, for example, even people with criminal records can easily obtain arms permits, if they bribe the relevant officials.[273]

Those who are **authorised users of weapons** are often suppliers of weapons. There are many cases of police, military, and private security companies selling or hiring their arms for personal gain. In Colombia, rogue elements of the police obtain arms through confiscation and may try to sell them back to the original owners.[275] In rural locations, such as some pastoralist areas of East Africa, the government may accept that it cannot provide security for its people, so it arms home-guards or police reservists, drawn from local populations, to protect their communities. People are seldom given adequate training or guidelines on how to use the weapons issued to them, and these arms are not usually provided equally to different ethnic groups, a fact which creates fear and tension.

Bad **weapons management** means that unauthorised users can acquire weapons. Huge quantities of arms are stolen from military or police depots. In Georgia, Russian stockpiles were looted systematically in 1991 and 1992, and those responsible were partly motivated by a belief that such actions were officially sanctioned as Soviet property became nationalised.[276] Arms are stolen from licensed shops and private individuals; in South Africa, where the two major sources of illegal firearms are loss and theft from licensed firearm owners and the state, 80 guns a day were reported lost or stolen in 1998.[277] In the Solomon Islands, the Malaita Eagle Force twice raided police armouries in 2000, obtaining enough M-18 assault rifles to commit, with police complicity, widespread violations of human rights against unarmed civilians from Guadalcanal Island.[278]

Supplier countries unwilling to help the recipients of their arms

Rio is one of the most violent states in Brazil, a country with one of the highest rates of firearms-related death in the world. Where do these weapons come from? Of 225,000 guns confiscated by the police in Rio de Janeiro State in 50 years, the majority were domestically produced, although they may well have left Brazil and re-entered the country via Paraguay. Of the weapons produced outside Brazil, the countries of origin (in descending order) were as follows: the USA (about 12,700), Spain (about 10,100), Belgium, Argentina, Germany, Italy, Czech Republic, Austria, France, China, Israel, Russia, and Switzerland.

In July 2002, Brazil asked for international co-operation to trace the routes of the weapons in order to curb their flow into the notoriously crime-ridden state. So far there has been a deafening silence from all foreign countries involved, with the exceptions of Argentina and Germany.[279]

'The Georgian soldiers used to give bullets to kids to play with, and if you gave them some vodka or cigarettes, they'd give you anything – a small gun or a grenade.'

Georgi, 14 years old, originally from Abkhazia in Georgia, but now displaced, 2000[274]

Embargo-busting arms flows to Iraq

During the 1980s, companies from Canada, China, France, Germany, Greece, the UK, and the USA provided military and 'dual use' technologies to companies and armed forces in Iraq.[281]

In 1990, after Iraq's invasion of Kuwait, a UN arms embargo was imposed. Despite this, Iraq continued to receive illegal arms supplies, much of it from newly independent states in Eastern and Central Europe.[282]

For example, it was reported that artillery, military vehicles and ammunition were supplied from the Federal Republic of Yugoslavia, artillery and munitions were supplied from Bosnia-Herzegovina and armoured vehicles were supplied from Bulgaria, despite evidence of indiscriminate military attacks using such equipment on Iraqi civilians.

During **conflict**, arms pass between warring parties as territory is won and lost, arms stores are captured and recaptured, and arms are abandoned on the battlefield. For many months, arms from Taliban caches discovered by US forces in Afghanistan were distributed freely to local militia.[283] As conflicts come to a close and peace agreements are signed, arms are often not collected from combatants and removed from society; instead, they move into civilian ownership; this was markedly the case in and around Mozambique and Cambodia. In Bosnia, seven years after the end of the war and after extensive weapons-collection exercises, NATO peacekeepers have said that most households possess some wartime weapon.[284] One million illegal weapons are still circulating in the Balkans region.[285]

In summary

It is clear that the lack of controls means that arms too easily get into the hands of those who use them to violate international human rights and humanitarian law – whether the abuser is an agent of a repressive government, a criminal, a violent husband, or a member of an armed political group. Some of the methods of transfer described above are 'legal' under the national laws of the states involved – because a law to control the transfer either does not exist or it has loopholes; but the fact that transfers are not banned does not make them morally right, and they may well be unlawful according to international law.

Chapter 5
Solutions at all levels

Photography: Crispin Hughes/Oxfam

UNAMSIL disarmament programme in Sierra Leone. A container-load of destroyed weapons from rebels and anti-government groups.

5: Solutions at all levels

'Arma Não! Ela Ou Eu'
– 'Choose gun free!
It's your weapon or me.'

Slogan of the women's anti-gun
campaign in Brazil

Solutions exist – but what about the political will to apply them?

▶ In some regions, arms policy has improved, but practice is still disastrously inadequate.

▶ The UN small-arms process is taking two steps forward and one step back.

▶ To prevent further abuses, it is necessary to stop the flow of new arms and to drain the pool of arms already in use in suffering communities.

▶ An Arms Trade Treaty is desperately needed, in order to ban all arms transfers which could lead to violations of international human rights and humanitarian law.

▶ National and regional arms controls also need to be strengthened in order to stop such transfers.

▶ Governments need to be more accountable to their citizens in their provision of protection from armed violence.

▶ Governments and civil society need to work together to improve safety at the community level.

The world has reached a critical point. Millions of arms are in circulation. They can be found in almost every corner of the world. They are often used to commit gross violations of international human rights and humanitarian law. Millions of people are suffering the consequences. Government action is required now. Governments have an obligation to protect their own citizens, but also to do what they can to prevent human rights abuses and war crimes abroad. This must involve working to stem the flow of arms and to stop arms abuse.

Some steps in the right direction

Over the last five years, the problem of the *illicit* proliferation of small arms has been acknowledged, and the political landscape has begun to change at the international level through the initiative of the UN. However, progress has been patchy, and the state-sanctioned arms trade has been ignored.

▶ Almost 10 years ago, 52 of the world's most powerful arms-exporting states signed up to the **Principles Governing Conventional Arms Transfers**. However, the practices of these states – all participants in the Organization for Security and Co-operation in Europe (OSCE) – fall far short of their agreed benchmark.

▶ More recently, the **European Union Code of Conduct on Arms Exports** stipulated that arms should not be exported to countries where there is a clear risk that they might be used for internal repression, external aggression or where serious violations of human rights have occurred. However, evidence cited in many independent reports suggests that this promise is not being fully kept.

▶ Since 2001, OSCE countries have been developing **'Best Practice Guidelines'** for the export and control of small arms and light weapons.[286]

There are still no binding laws or regulatory requirements that oblige arms-exporting states to respect international human rights or humanitarian law when authorising the transfer of arms or military, security, and police training services to other countries. Even where human rights criteria are referred to, they are often loosely interpreted. In particular, when governments consider proposed exports, inadequate attention is paid to the long lifecycle of most types of arms and security equipment and technology – and hence to the prolonged risk of abuse.

What is needed is a genuine commitment by all governments to enact powerful new arms-control laws, consistent with international human rights standards and humanitarian law, which will bring an end to their complicity in the abuse of small arms.

The UN and small arms

There have been two steps forward towards international controls on small arms since 2000, both addressing the illicit trade in arms. First, the UN Firearms Protocol has been agreed. This is concerned with the illicit manufacture and trafficking of firearms by criminal organisations. As of March 2003, the Protocol had been signed by 52 states but ratified by only three, hence it is unlikely to enter into force for some years.[288] Second, a Programme of Action to Prevent, Combat and Eradicate the Illicit Trade in Small Arms and Light Weapons in All its Aspects was agreed at a UN conference in July 2001. After an implementation meeting in 2003, where there was no consensus on moving forward, there will be another in 2005, followed by a review conference in 2006.

The Programme of Action contains several positive provisions, such as specific measures against which to monitor progress on issues such as the collection and destruction of arms, and the management of stockpiles. However the 2001 UN Conference did not achieve more than very general commitments, and it was in many ways a wasted opportunity. The US and Russian governments joined with

'[Small arms and light] weapons have prolonged or aggravated conflicts, produced massive flows of refugees, undermined the rule of law and spawned a culture of violence and impunity. In short, the excessive accumulation and illicit trade of small arms is threatening international peace and security, dashing hopes for social and economic development, and jeopardising prospects for democracy and human rights.'

Kofi Annan, UN Secretary-General, 2002[287]

those of China and some in the Non-Aligned Movement to weaken the UN Programme of Action significantly. Specifically, they prevented the conference from addressing the misuse of arms, especially when referring to state agents, despite overwhelming evidence of the problems caused by such misuse.[289] The Programme of Action does not mention human rights, and there are few references to international humanitarian law, nor does it provide any mandate for the negotiation of a binding instrument.

In relation to the global threat, the progress is proceeding at a frustratingly slow pace. The UN's first step towards reform of the trade in small arms and light weapons must not remain the only step to control the global flow of conventional arms.

Stop the flow and drain the pool

The excessive and uncontrolled proliferation of arms must be tackled by the following measures:

▶ Preventing the flow of arms used to commit abuses, by stronger controls on the movement of arms.

▶ Taking arms out of communities which are already awash with weapons, and reducing the availability of arms and the likelihood of their being misused.

Stop the flow of arms

Controlling the flow of weapons into a country is a critical step. The right of states to arm for self-defence comes with an international legal and moral responsibility to control the weapons and ensure that they are used appropriately. Similarly, the duty of states to regulate the sale of arms must be taken seriously.

It is vital that governments do not authorise the transfer of arms if there are grounds to believe there is a risk that they will be used for grave violations of international human rights or humanitarian law, or where the proliferation of arms undermines sustainable development.

Governments must also tighten controls to stop the flow of illicit weapons. This means ensuring that embargoes are not broken, that brokers are regulated, and that arms smuggling is prevented.

The primary responsibility for the flow of arms into a country rests with governments – *all* governments that export, re-export, or import arms.

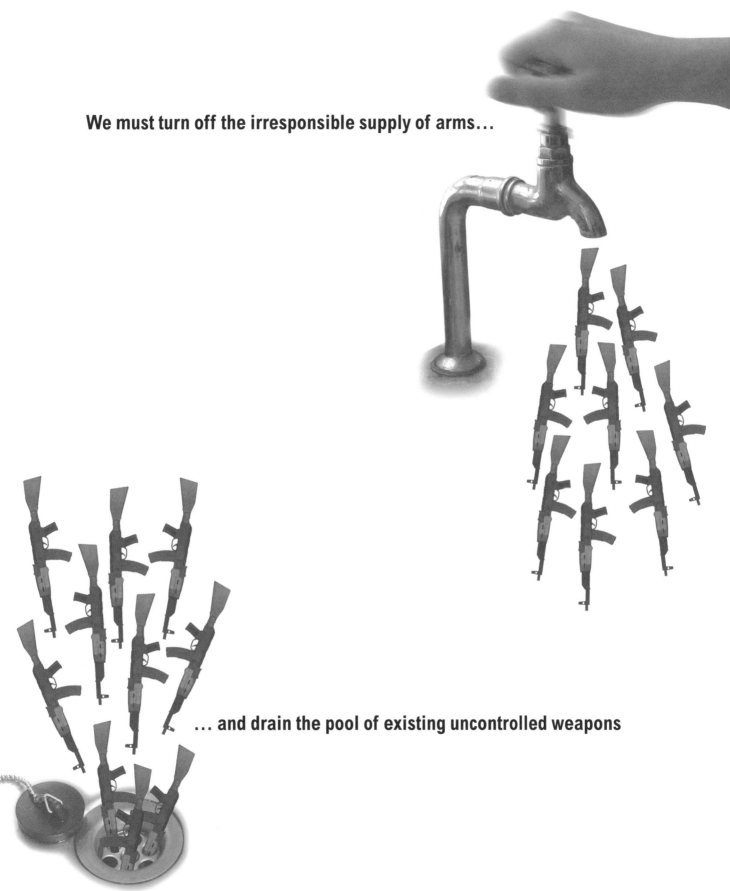

We must turn off the irresponsible supply of arms…

… and drain the pool of existing uncontrolled weapons

Strong controls on arms are needed to reduce the likelihood of war, crime, and repression, to diminish their scope and impact should they occur, and to reduce the political and economic costs of armed violence.[291] Such controls already have a firm basis in existing international law and standards – human rights law, international humanitarian law, and norms on sustainable development. Oxfam and Amnesty International are calling for these controls to be applied directly and clearly to the transfer and use of arms.

However, in isolation, these critical measures will have little impact. Even if all irresponsible transfers ceased tomorrow, many state forces and communities already possess large quantities of arms, under such minimal control that the risk of abuse would remain high for years to come.

Drain the pool of arms

Armed violence is not inevitable. Arms must be strictly limited and controlled by establishing a rigorous system of accountability and training, and removing illegal and surplus weapons from communities gravely affected by armed violence. This is a simple concept, but arms can be strictly controlled and collected effectively only when an environment is created which fosters the peaceful resolution of conflict, the responsible and legitimate use of arms, and confidence in the prospect of non-armed security. Governments, security services, the judiciary, community leaders, and civilian users of guns must work together and take action to reduce the means and motive for armed violence.

That means, above all, that all state actors entitled to use arms must strictly follow the 26 provisions of the UN Basic Principles on the Use of Force and Firearms and, when necessary, the provisions of the Geneva Conventions and other relevant international humanitarian laws. All of these provisions must be incorporated into domestic state laws in every country, and guaranteed by means of rigorous training and monitoring.

Although complex and challenging, the task of controlling the proliferation and misuse of small arms is not impossible, and models of good practice already exist:

▶ Programmes of weapons collection and destruction have developed significantly over the past 10 years. They now incorporate development-related incentives, whereby recompense for the surrendered weapons assists the rebuilding of communities.

▶ South African civil society has led the way in the designation of schools, hospitals, public buildings, and even towns as Gun Free Zones, thus reducing fear and armed violence.

'If only the enemy would listen, it would have been wonderful, and the firing would stop and we would listen to each other, we would just talk and try not to use guns. I wish we could end all this violence and we could develop our country.'

Girl soldier, the Philippines, 2001[292]

74

▶ The Sierra Leonean government involved civil society in plans for reconstituting the armed forces and incorporating training and education on principles of democratic governance and human rights, and international humanitarian law.[293]

An international initiative: the Arms Trade Treaty

Arms producers have a right to sell, and others have a right to buy, but rights confer responsibilities and legal obligations.

The fact that an arms transfer is 'authorised' by state officials does not mean that it is necessarily a lawful act. A 'legal' arms transfer is often interpreted by governments to mean 'lawful under national laws'. However, to be fully legal, a transfer must also be lawful under international law. The UN Disarmament Commission clearly recognises this distinction and has defined illicit transfers as 'that international trade in conventional arms which is contrary to the laws of states and/or international law'. This was endorsed in July 2001 by the UN Conference on small arms.

But what are these obligations under international law? The proposed Arms Trade Treaty (ATT) sets out principles based upon existing responsibilities of states under international standards.[295] It pulls together relevant international laws and standards which should apply to international arms transfers – such as the Geneva Conventions, the Mine Ban Treaty, and the Convention against Genocide. It is a simple, clear document which defines the criteria against which any proposed transfer of conventional arms should be permitted. It would require states to incorporate these criteria into their national law and to make regular public reports of all arms transferred to an international registry. (See Appendix 1 for more details on international law and arms.)

The Arms Trade Treaty codifies the principle that arms exports are in breach of international law if the exporter has knowledge, or ought reasonably to have knowledge, that the arms will be used for violations of international human rights or humanitarian law.[296] Knowledge by relevant state officials that arms are likely to be used for such grave violations introduces a responsibility to prevent such a transfer, especially from that state's own territory or jurisdiction.[297] Therefore any state exporting weapons – not merely newly manufactured arms, but re-exported, second-hand weapons too – has clear responsibilities to ensure that the weapons are used in a manner consistent with standards already agreed under international law. The exporting state would be required to monitor closely what happens once the arms left its borders, since the manner in which the recipient state will use the weapons may affect the lawfulness of the transfer.

'The availability and misuse of [small arms and light] weapons has an indisputable impact on the number, type and gravity of violations of international human rights and humanitarian law committed by state and non-state actors.'

Barbara Frey, UN Special Rapporteur on Small Arms[294]

The Arms Trade Treaty – if widely accepted – will establish a firm and unambiguous international mechanism to prohibit the sale of weapons where there is a clear risk that those weapons will be used for serious abuses.

The Arms Trade Treaty would be an **international** means of control, to ensure that all nations are working to the same standard. National and regional systems are extremely important in combating illicit transfers; they provide a critical level of control and are the primary safeguard against irresponsible transfers. However, they are not mutually consistent, and some contain ambiguities and loopholes which make it easy for illicit dealers to ply their trade. For example, there have been numerous cases of questionable arms transfers through Slovakia, because there are no functioning controls over arms in transit;[299] in the Netherlands, where there is little arms production but major arms transhipments, items from 'friendly' countries are exempted from certain mandatory licences, and items in 'fast transit' need no licence at all.[300] The Arms Trade Treaty would also help to ensure that deals rejected by one supplier are not picked up by another, thus preventing a situation similar to that in late 2002, when, despite Germany's refusal to sell rifles to the Nepalese government on human rights grounds, Belgium supplied them instead.

What would be legal and illegal under the ATT

Legal transfer
Small arms sold to a police force, where they are used in line with the Basic Principles on the Use of Force and Firearms

Illegal transfer
The same arms sold to a police force which is undisciplined and corrupt, which uses arms for extra-judicial killings and torture

Legal transfer
Military aircraft and armoured personnel carriers sold to governments for use in an army fully abiding by international humanitarian law

Illegal transfer
The same arms sold to governments where they are used to target civilians instead of military objectives

The Arms Trade Treaty would be **legally binding**. The regional politically binding instruments that exist currently are not legally enforceable. Difficult decisions are, at the end of the day, merely subject to the judgement of political representatives or civil servants. The Arms Trade Treaty, however, fosters a culture of compliance by creating a permanent legal connection between arms and abuses; and it brings arms-export standards into line with existing responsibilities under international law.

Even though some countries are opposed to an ATT, this should not prevent other states from forging ahead. Although not all countries have signed the Mine Ban Treaty (prohibiting anti-personnel mines), a new international norm has been created by means of worldwide pressure and campaigning. Since this treaty came into force, not a single country has openly traded anti-personnel landmines, far fewer governments are using anti-personnel landmines, and even some non-signatories are broadly abiding by its principles.[301]

Core principles of the Arms Trade Treaty

Article 1: Principle – All international arms transfers should be authorised by the appropriate state authority.

Article 2: Express limitations – Governments have a responsibility to ensure that transfers do not directly violate their obligations under international law: This includes:
a. transfer of particular types of weapon – if they are indiscriminate or are of a nature to cause superfluous injury or unnecessary suffering;
b. transfer to particular countries – if covered by embargoes.

Article 3: Limitations based on anticipated use – Governments have a responsibility to ensure that the weapons they transfer are not used illegally. The transfer must not proceed if there is knowledge that the arms will be:
a. used for breaches of the UN charter, particularly the use of force in international relations;
b. used for serious violations of human rights, international humanitarian law, genocide, crimes against humanity; or
c. diverted and used to commit any of the above.

Article 4: Other issues to take into account – Governments have a responsibility not to transfer arms if the arms are likely to:
a. be used for or to facilitate the commission of violent crimes;
b. adversely affect political stability or regional security;
c. adversely affect sustainable development; or
d. be diverted and used to commit any of the above.

The current form of the treaty addresses only government-authorised transfers, but protocols for brokering and licensed production will also be produced. These will apply the same principles, ensuring that government authorisation for brokering and licensed production are based on the criteria for arms transfers outlined above.

Consensus is already growing in support of the Arms Trade Treaty:

▶ It has a compelling **legal basis**: the proposed text draws on existing and emerging obligations of states under international law.

▶ There is a powerful **moral justification** to refuse some arms deals. It is never right to supply weapons which will be used to commit atrocities, even if other less responsible countries are willing to do it. Establishing this principle internationally would put the onus on non-compliant arms exporters to justify their practices.

'Getting a commitment through international law made a real difference over landmines. It made governments responsible for change.'

Comment from a participant in an NGO workshop on small arms in Nairobi, 2001[302]

▶ There is a clear **political mandate**. Under the Programme of Action from the UN Conference on small arms, states agreed 'to assess applications for export authorizations according to strict national regulations and procedures that cover all categories of small arms and light weapons and are *consistent with States' existing responsibilities under international law...*'.[303]

Regional initiatives: essential building blocks

Although little progress has been made on the control of heavy weapons at the regional level, the problem of small arms has been discussed in regional forums all over the world. There is an emerging consensus that more resolute action is required. Regional actions have varied widely, from legislative instruments to a broader commitment for further action.

Different mechanisms have different strengths. For example:

▶ **European Union: The Code of Conduct on Arms Exports** (1998) prevents the export of conventional weapons to destinations where they might lead to internal repression and external aggression. A key strength is its mechanism to prevent 'undercutting' – to stop one country agreeing to supply arms, if the request has already been rejected by another. Although not perfect, this is a powerful mechanism, because it encourages transparency between suppliers and goes some way to ensuring compliance.

▶ **The Americas: The Inter-American Convention against Illicit Manufacturing and Trafficking and Model Regulations for the Control of International Movement of Firearms** (1997/8) are two instruments covering firearms, ammunition, and explosives in the context of law enforcement and crime control. The Convention will be the only legally binding regional agreement on small arms, once it has entered into force; as of May 2003, 20 out of 34 states had ratified it.[305] However, it does not require states to assess arms-export applications against normative criteria such as principles of human rights or international humanitarian law.

▶ **West Africa: The Moratorium on the Import, Export and Manufacture of Small Arms and Light Weapons** (1998) is the world's first regional moratorium on small arms. The importation of new weapons is prohibited without approval from other member states. This ban is supported by the largest group of arms-exporting states (the Wassennaar Arrangement). Although strong in principle, this political commitment has been violated by several countries, including Liberia and Côte d'Ivoire.

► **Great Lakes and the Horn of Africa: Nairobi Declaration on the Problem of the Proliferation of Illicit Small Arms and Light Weapons** (2000) includes a requirement for countries to develop national action plans to address arms-related issues; Tanzania's has been completed, Uganda's and Kenya's are in development. It also explicitly recognises the role of civil society.

These and other similar agreements are an important first step in developing a regional approach to tackle arms proliferation, fostering co-operation, trust, and information exchange among governments. While some are poorly implemented, primarily owing to lack of political will, they remain key drivers for further initiatives to reduce the transfer of arms into the regions and between neighbouring countries.

However, the effectiveness of current regional arms controls is limited by four evident weaknesses:

► They do not expressly include provisions that legally uphold existing responsibilities under international law.

► Most are only politically binding, not legally binding, with the result that they are more difficult to enforce.

► Many apply only to illicit arms for use in criminal operations and ignore state-sanctioned arms transfers.

► They generally do not address the major loopholes being exploited by unscrupulous arms dealers, namely the lack of control of arms brokers and transporters, and of foreign licensed production.

There is therefore significant scope to strengthen the arms controls, drawing together best practice from the agreements that already exist, and making explicit reference to existing responsibilities relating to international human rights and humanitarian law. Already, for example, NGOs in the Americas are working to promote a regional instrument based upon international human rights and humanitarian law. Similar processes are beginning in other regions.

National initiatives: the duty of the state to protect its citizens

The inherent right to life and security is something special. It underpins the UN Charter, is enshrined in the Universal Declaration of Human Rights, and codified into law in the International Covenant on Civil and Political Rights. The role of the state is to provide safety and security, to protect its citizens and safeguard this right, through government and national institutions.

'This belief in disarmament does not proceed from idealism or from naïveté. The best strategy for prevention of armed conflict is to eliminate the means of violence.'

Alpha Oumar Konaré, former President of Mali.[306]

As this report shows, when it comes to arms control, too often this protection is not provided. Lack of effective arms control by a state may result in a direct threat by force of arms to a person's safety, or a threat to his or her means of survival or security. A change of state policy and practice to control the flow and use of arms is vital if this threat is to be removed.

Arms transfers

Governments must lead the way in implementing national export controls which are based on international human rights and humanitarian law. The criteria as defined in the Arms Trade Treaty provide the benchmark for such controls.
In addition to export controls, concerted steps should be taken to close two of the main international loopholes exploited by arms manufacturers, dealers, brokers, and traffickers.

▶ There should be strict national registration of each arms manufacturer, broker, transporter, and financier, even if they operate only through 'third countries'. Those convicted of criminal offences involving money laundering, trafficking, and firearms-related violence should be removed from the register.[308]

▶ Licences for export, transit, and import should be controlled on a case-by-case basis, and should include full details of the brokers, transporters, and financiers involved. They should be issued by the sending, receiving, and transit governments after direct consultation with each other and with the home governments of any brokers, transporters, and financiers involved, and they should be issued only if the arms transfers proposed will not reach anyone likely to violate international human rights and humanitarian law.

Civilian arms ownership and violent crime

The UN has expressed its concern about the high incidence of crimes, accidents, and suicides involving the civilian misuse of firearms, noting the lack of appropriate regulations in many countries for their possession and storage, and the lack of training in the use of firearms.[309] Among the countries identified by the UN as having very high firearm deaths per 100,000 people were Colombia (55.85), Brazil (26.97), Jamaica (18.72), and the USA (14.05). These contrast with much lower rates in Japan (0.07), the UK (0.46), Spain (0.70), the Netherlands (0.74) and Denmark (0.80).[310]

There is growing pressure to hold states accountable for violent crimes, and to punish any state's failure to establish reasonable regulation regarding the private ownership of small arms; failure to protect individuals from domestic violence; and failure to protect individuals from organised crime, including kidnapping for ransom.[311]

Under international human rights law, every person has a duty to respect another's right to life.[312] More importantly, states have a duty to take positive measures to prevent acts of violence and unlawful killings, including those committed by private persons.[313] There is growing recognition that states' duties under international human rights law include exercising due diligence to ensure that basic rights – certainly the right to life and security of the person – are not abused by private actors.[314] Where a foreseeable consequence of a failure to exercise adequate control over the civilian possession and use of arms is continued or increased violence, then states might be held liable for this failure under international human rights law.

In situations where civilian possession and abuse of firearms is controlled weakly or not at all, police officers have expressed concern that it is difficult to protect the public.[315] According to international standards, law-enforcement officers should 'as far as possible, apply non-violent means before resorting to the use of force and firearms' and then 'only if other means remain ineffective'. This task becomes increasingly difficult where possession and use of guns is spiralling out of control.[316] The UN Basic Principles also require states to establish a legal framework and effective system to regulate the control, storage, and issuing of firearms and ammunition to law-enforcement officers.

In addition, the Basic Principles require states to 'prohibit the use of those firearms and ammunition that cause unwarranted injury or present an unwarranted risk', which in many countries is taken to mean that military-specification weapons should not normally be used for policing. It would appear to follow logically that such weapons should certainly not be in civilian possession.[317]

Even governments with minimal resources have begun to take concerted action to combat violent crime, including measures to strictly control the civilian possession of firearms. In Malawi, for example, the Chamber of Commerce and other civil-society organisations publicly criticised the government in 1999 for not doing enough to stem the rise of armed crime, and the government has since, with UK aid, expanded its national programme to reform the police and has engaged community organisations in Community Policing Forums to help to fight violent crime and counter the illegal possession of firearms.[318]

'Please remember my son Matthew and all the children and young people who have died or been injured and traumatised around this world. Remember that they were denied the basic right to live their lives.'

Mary Leigh Blek, President of the Million Mom March, USA, speech to the UN conference on small arms, 2001

Local initiatives: building safer communities

Increasing safety at the community level is inextricably bound up with the reasons why people hold and resort to arms. The primary reason for villagers in Afghanistan, Yemen, and Switzerland to hold weapons will differ radically: respectively, to protect themselves against armed groups, as a cultural symbol and an expression of their constitutional right, or to defend their country from armed attack. But there will be other aspects too – and these multiple and interconnecting motives for bearing arms must be fully understood.

Building government capacity to protect citizens in Kenya

In Kenya, particularly northern Kenya, armed violence is widespread. This problem cannot be solved without major changes in policy and practice at the government level, supported by community action and advocacy. Weapons collection and durable disarmament have little chance of succeeding when communities feel the need to arm themselves to maintain their security.

Many NGOs, including Oxfam and Amnesty International, are campaigning at the national level to promote a comprehensive, inclusive, and participatory process of security-sector reform. The state's capacity to protect its citizens based on international human rights standards must be developed; immediate measures should include the following:

- the development of community-based policing, with local consultation on the nature and quality of policing and security, and community oversight over existing structures;
- a review of existing local security structures, such as police reservists and other militia, in order to assess their appropriateness, effectiveness, and degree of accountability;
- most critically, reasonable remuneration and benefits for the police and other security forces, along with effective training, accountability, and civilian oversight, to reduce corruption and increase professionalism.

Therefore measures to address community safety cannot be generalised. They may be concerned less with the weapons themselves and more with the complex web of social, cultural, political, and economic conditions that shape demand and use. Work at the local level must include specific programmes to improve community safety, in the following ways.

1. Rebuilding confidence in the possibility of non-armed security through

▶ reducing the quantity of arms in circulation, by means of weapons collection and destruction programmes, the establishment of gun-free zones, and removing illegal arms which could contribute to violations of human rights and humanitarian law;

▶ building relationships and trust between differing communities and between communities and police;

▶ delivering civic education and awareness-raising programmes;

▶ introducing the culture and tools for peaceful conflict resolution; a model is provided by the NGO Viva Rio in Rio de Janeiro, Brazil, which, together with the Justice Department, has implemented 'Civil Rights Counters', which provide free legal assistance and support for conflict resolution.

2. Providing assistance to the victims of armed violence. There is no system for support to victims of armed violence, unlike the case of landmine victims, yet gun-related injuries and deaths damage the economy and well-being of whole families.

3. Developing sustainable livelihoods as alternatives to armed violence. Too often the possession of arms is perceived as a route to economic survival.

Although it is impossible to prescribe solutions to increase community safety, experience reveals some **guiding principles for work at the community level**.

1. *Detailed analysis and understanding* of the community and its governance are essential, in order to identify the main reasons why people bear arms. The research should include all stakeholders, and particularly people in power and authority, such as the police.

2. A *holistic view* of the situation must be taken, which will probably involve addressing all human rights issues, including poverty, justice and the problem of impunity for offenders. Reform of, or at least collaboration with, policing and criminal-justice systems based on international human rights standards are necessary. Alternatives to using guns to establish livelihoods must be considered.

3. *Genuine engagement of the community* is imperative. Initiatives must be driven by local people, to ensure relevance, ownership, participation, shared responsibility, and understanding. Political representatives and the police must be representative, accountable, and responsive to the community as a whole.

4. The needs, perspectives, and talents of *all members of the community* need to be incorporated. This includes men, women, girls, boys, older people, people with disabilities, and people of different ethnicities and religions. For example, former

'Apartheid policing broke down community trust of the state. Under the new democratic government, crime escalated – we saw running gun battles between gangs – until community-based policing took root. After four years, we have solved over 500 murder cases, recovered stolen vehicles and confiscated illegal weapons – AK-47s, handguns, shotguns, rifles and home-made pipe-guns. Police officers are responding rapidly to community reports, trying to avoid the use of firearms.'

Captain Pillay, Police Special Investigations Task Team, Edendale, South Africa, 2002[320]

combatants and gang members from different sides may have much in common and can act powerfully for change in challenging 'machismo' values and gun culture, while for young people, alternatives must be found to substitute for the benefits of gang membership, such as a sense of identity, purpose, group support, and security.

5. *Partnership between civil society and government* is a key factor. Civil society is essential for achieving constructive change, but sustainable change of policy and practice also requires government involvement. Governments can be strong allies – endorsing, strengthening, and sustaining the movement for reform – but civil society should be careful to avoid co-option and inducements to legitimise inappropriate government policy. Effective flows of information are critical to ensure effective co-operation.

Building relationships between communities in Sri Lanka

Sri Lanka has experienced an unmanageable proliferation of arms – including sophisticated weapons on sale at low prices – in its communities. Armed violence, triggered by freely available weapons, has resulted in forced displacement and a drastic decline in socio-economic status, income sources, expenditure patterns, and health care. One major impact is fear – fear of attacks by the security forces or armed opposition groups.

The current ceasefire between government forces and rebel groups has created new opportunities and challenges for building peace. Oxfam is working with neighbouring communities to rebuild community relationships. Safe space must be provided in which people can interact peacefully, building trust and understanding, and addressing tensions without resorting to armed violence. There is a particular need to focus on the young, who until now have been exposed almost exclusively to military ideologies and aspirations; this can be achieved through innovative social programmes, building relationships among young people from different ethnic groups.

Improved weapons management in Cambodia
(based on the experience of the Working Group for Weapons Reduction, Phnom Penh)

Arms have diffused into communities in Cambodia during almost 30 years of internal armed conflict. Handguns and military assault rifles in private hands are common in both rural and urban areas: numbers are estimated at between 500,000 and one million. According to a 1998 survey, at least two thirds of households in Phnom Penh possessed illicit weapons. The proliferation of weapons has contributed to widespread public fear and insecurity, and the culture of violence is increasingly evident as weapons are used with impunity in domestic disputes, traffic incidents, and attempts at self-protection.

A key priority is weapons management. Weapons from earlier collections were stored in poorly secured and unsafe state warehouses, from where they were illegally sold and re-circulated. More effective weapons-storage depots and tight monitoring must be provided for the police at provincial and district levels, so that all collected arms and those in police hands will be stored safely and responsibly. Secondly, the registration and control of police weapons must be improved to prevent 'leakage' from security forces into civilian hands. The process of issuing licences through the Ministry of the Interior, and particularly the police, must also be restricted.

However, all these local initiatives are far more likely to succeed if the flood of weapons from abroad is replaced by an effectively controlled supply of arms which are genuinely needed and will not fuel further abuses. In other words, actions at all levels – from local to global – must reinforce each other. The five permanent members of the UN Security Council must control their own supplies; former Soviet Bloc countries must control the dispersal of their surpluses, and all countries must agree the Arms Trade Treaty as the new global measure to control all arms transfers.

6: The time for action is now

All governments must take responsible and concerted action to control the proliferation, possession, and misuse of arms, in line with international law. The irresponsible use and transfer of arms is neither inevitable nor in the interests of states. The lack of national and international controls on arms has led to a catastrophic proliferation of supply, which in turn is fuelling conflict, state repression, and crime, undermining development and conflict-resolution efforts, and increasing the lethality of disputes. These impacts are engendering poverty and suffering, and they cannot be allowed to continue. Something must change.

Governments have the authority and obligation both to ensure the security and rights of their citizens and to manage arms transfers so that the rights of people in other countries are not abused. Therefore it is primarily their responsibility to solve this problem. This must be done in close collaboration with civil society – in developing strategy, implementing programmes, and sharing information – and, where necessary, in collaboration with donors and external providers of expertise.

Not only would such action save lives and improve the conditions of daily existence for millions, it would also demonstrate that nations retain faith in the ability of multilateral bodies to act vigorously in the interests of ordinary people, particularly the poorest men, women, and children around the world.

International action

At the international level, governments should:

1. **Adopt the Arms Trade Treaty** by the time of the 2006 UN review conference on small arms. Progressive governments must champion the Arms Trade Treaty in international and regional forums and lobby other governments, pressing for action outside the UN process if necessary. Once in force, this new legally binding treaty will ensure that all states are working to the same standard, to prevent the irresponsible transfer of arms where they would contribute to violations of international human rights and humanitarian law.

2. **Create new international instruments to prevent irresponsible arms brokering, transporting and financing, and foreign licensed production,** using the Arms Trade Treaty criteria to define and prevent irresponsible transfers.

3. **Provide more funding for practical assistance** for arms-affected communities – particularly from donor agencies in arms-producing countries.

Regional action

At the regional level, neighbouring governments must work together to:

1. **Create or strengthen regional arms controls**, based upon international human rights and humanitarian law, building on – as well as inspiring – work at the national level. Such controls should both address the flow of arms, instituting effective measures to limit supply and reduce demand for weapons, and also reduce the widespread availability of arms, striving to improve community safety. Regional collaboration provides opportunities for sharing information and best practice, as well as building consensus on regional policies and programmes.

National action

At the national level, every government must act responsibly to prevent the misuse of arms:

1. Ensure the **responsible use of arms by its security forces,** based firmly on existing international human rights standards and principles of humanitarian law, requiring a minimum level of training, discipline, and control. All states should abide by the UN Basic Principles for the Use of Force and Firearms by Law Enforcement Officials, the UN Code of Conduct for Law Enforcement Officials, the Geneva Conventions and other relevant international standards, incorporating their provisions into domestic law in every country.

2. **Take swift action, when conflict has ended,** to work with international bodies to implement high-quality disarmament, demobilisation, and reintegration programmes.

3. **Establish independent mechanisms to bring to justice,** without delay, those who perpetrate serious violations of international human rights or humanitarian law, ensuring that such violations are adequately punished and other steps are taken to end impunity.

4. **Enforce existing legislation or create new legislation** to control the import, export, transit, production, management, and use of all arms. The standards outlined in the Arms Trade Treaty should be used when taking decisions on national arms exports, ensuring that human rights, international humanitarian law, and sustainable development do not suffer under commercial pressure.

5. **Ensure transparency and oversight** by providing regular and meaningful information to the public about the production, possession, and transfer of arms. These reports should be subject to regular review by legislatures and parliaments.

6. **With civil society, develop and implement an action plan for the strict control of all arms.** A first step is to undertake a broad review to assess problems of protection, arms availability, and misuse of weapons; then to develop solutions and implement an effective action plan. Each stage must involve close collaboration with civil society.

Local action

Community safety must be improved by the following means:

1. Rebuild confidence in the possibility of non-armed security, by

▶ **reducing the quantity of surplus and illegal arms in circulation** – through the establishment of gun-free zones, removal of illegal arms which could contribute to violations of international human rights and humanitarian law, and destruction of surplus weapons;

▶ **building relationships and trust** between opposing communities and between communities and police; such work should be based on international human rights and humanitarian standards;

▶ **delivering civic education about community safety** to counter cultures of violence, including the destructive link between arms and conventional notions of masculinity;

▶ **introducing and using tools for peaceful conflict resolution.**

2. **Providing assistance** to victims of armed violence.

3. **Developing sustainable livelihoods as an alternative** for those who might be dependent upon armed violence for their living.

To date, there has been a tragic lack of urgency on the part of most governments around the world to address the problem of the proliferation of arms. Words are plentiful, real progress is slight. The time to act is now.

Civil society and governments need to work proactively and effectively together to address the problem of arms at each level – stemming the source of the supply, and addressing the reasons why people possess arms in insecure environments.

Oxfam, Amnesty International, and IANSA (the International Action Network on Small Arms, which represents more than 500 non-government organisations around the world) are campaigning for a safer future for us all, through strong action to turn the tide of weapons abuse. Certain key governments have already expressed their support for this work, and we appeal to others to join our efforts.

Appendix 1 – The legal basis for work on the regulation of armaments

The UN Charter contains two very important articles relating to arms:

▶ Article 26: 'In order to promote the establishment and maintenance of international peace and security with the least diversion for armaments of the world's human and economic resources, the Security Council shall be responsible for formulating, with the assistance of the Military Staff Committee referred to in Article 47, plans to be submitted to the Members of the United Nations for the establishment of a system for the regulation of armaments.'

▶ Article 51: 'Nothing in the present Charter shall impair the inherent right of individual or collective self-defence if an armed attack occurs against a Member of the United Nations, until the Security Council has taken measures necessary to maintain international peace and security…'

International human rights law seeks to protect individual rights and freedoms. The Universal Declaration of Human Rights contains a number of articles which are directly relevant for limiting the use of arms and which are now generally regarded as binding in customary international law.[321] The key principles are: 'Everyone has the right to life, liberty and security of person', and 'No one shall be subjected to torture or to cruel, inhuman, degrading treatment or punishment'. Even where people are not killed or wounded directly by gunshot, the presence of an armed threat by agents of the state can facilitate other forms of violence, amounting to grave violations of human rights.

There are numerous international human rights treaties that create binding legal obligations on states party to them. One of the most important treaties ratified by about two thirds of all states, the International Covenant on Civil and Political Rights, states that 'No one shall be arbitrarily deprived of his life'. Governments must ensure that all agents of the state respect the right to life, and punish those who do not, but also act to ensure that the right is protected against threats by other actors, including private individuals. They must exercise due diligence to prevent acts of violence, including through effective policing. Certain rights can be waived in times of public emergency, but the right not to be arbitrarily deprived of life is 'non-derogable': states are bound to respect it fully in all circumstances.[322]

In addition to treaties, international human rights law includes many 'soft law' standards that states should follow. The UN Basic Principles for the Use of Force and Firearms by Law Enforcement Officials clearly state that firearms must be used only in certain limited circumstances, and only when less extreme means are insufficient. Most importantly, Basic Principle 9 states: 'In any event, intentional lethal use of firearms may only be made when strictly unavoidable in order to protect life.'[323]

International humanitarian law (IHL) seeks to limit and prevent human suffering in times of armed conflict. Even wars have rules. It applies to all parties to conflicts, including in civil wars to armed groups operating outside of state control. IHL attempts to place limits on the discretion of parties to choose methods of warfare, and aims to balance military necessity with humanitarian principles. International humanitarian law prohibits deliberate attacks on anyone who is not taking an active part in the armed conflict, whether civilian, prisoner, or wounded combatant, and prohibits indiscriminate or disproportionate attacks. Although the precise articles of the Geneva Conventions that apply depend on whether or not the conflict is international, the key principles are generally applicable in all types of armed conflict: a distinction must be made between combatants and non-combatants; the use of force must always be *proportional* to the intended military advantage; and taking adequate *precaution* to minimise incidental damage to civilians and civilian property and non-combatants is essential, before and during any military attack.[324]

The Rome Statute of the International Criminal Court restates customary international human rights norms, prohibiting crimes against humanity in peace time or war time (Art. 7), in addition to war crimes in both international and internal conflicts (Art. 8).

Selected sources of international human rights and humanitarian law that limit the transfer and misuse of small arms and light weapons

Situation	Examples of violations	Applicable law
1. Misuse of small arms by agents of the state	Genocide Intentional killings by security forces Excessive force by law enforcement Disproportionately violent government reaction to disturbances Systematic rape Torture Forced displacement Deprivation of basic human needs	Universal Declaration of Human Rights, Art. 3 International Covenant on Civil and Political Rights (ICCPR), Art. 4 (2) ICCPR, Art. 6 Convention on the Prevention and Punishment of the Crime of Genocide ('Genocide Convention') Code of Conduct for Law Enforcement Officials, Art. 3 Basic Principles on the Use of Force and Firearms by Law Enforcement Officials
2. Misuse of small arms by private persons when the state fails to exercise due diligence	Ethnic, religious, political killings or massacres Failure to prevent criminal homicide Failure to prevent domestic violence Failure to prevent crimes committed post-conflict by individual owners of small arms	Universal Declaration of Human Rights, Art. 3 ICCPR, Art. 6 'Due diligence' standard, Inter-American Court of Human Rights, European Court of Human Rights Declaration on the Right and Responsibility of Individuals, Groups and Organs of Society to Promote and Protect Universally Recognized Rights and Fundamental Freedoms, Art. 2 (1), Art. 2 (2)
3. Misuse of small arms by state agents in armed conflict	Genocide Extrajudicial executions or torture of non-combatants and prisoners of war Attacks on peacekeepers and humanitarian workers Collective punishments against civilian populations in situations of occupation Forcibly relocating civilian populations Using weapons that cause unnecessary suffering Summary executions of captured combatants Exploitation of children as soldiers Indiscriminate use of weapons Crimes against humanity, and war crimes	Treaty bans on specific weapons: St. Petersburg Declaration (1869) (exploding projectiles) The Hague Declaration (1899) (dum dum bullets) Geneva Conventions of 1949, Common Article 3 Additional Protocol II to the Geneva Conventions, and relating to the Protection of Victims of Non-International Armed Conflicts Genocide Convention Rome Statute of the International Criminal Court ICCPR, Art. 6, Art. 7 Convention on the Rights of the Child, Art. 38 Optional Protocol to the Convention on the Rights of the Child on the involvement of children in armed conflict
4. Misuse of small arms by opposition groups in armed conflict	Genocide Mass killings Systematic rape Attacks on civilians, peacekeepers and humanitarian workers Exploitation of children as soldiers Forced displacement of populations Hostage-taking	Geneva Conventions of 1949, Common Article 3 Additional Protocol II to the Geneva Conventions, and relating to the Protection of Victims of Non-International Armed Conflicts Genocide Convention Rome Statute of the International Criminal Court
5. Arms transfer with knowledge that arms are likely to be used to commit serious violations of international human rights and humanitarian law	Violation of UN Security Council arms embargoes Transfer to insurgent group in another state Transfer to a state identified as having a consistent pattern of gross and reliably attested violations of human rights and fundamental freedoms Transfer to a state that uses child soldiers Transfer to a state unable to control post-conflict violence Transfer to a state known to violate international humanitarian law norms in situations of armed conflict	UN Charter, Chapter VII (arms embargoes) Geneva Conventions of 1949, Common Article 1 UN Declaration on the Inadmissibility of Intervention in the Domestic Affairs of States and Protection of Their Independence and Sovereignty Declaration on the Enhancement of the Effectiveness of the Principle of Refraining from the Threat or Use of Force in International Relations International Law Commission, Draft articles on Responsibility of States for Internationally Wrongful Acts

Adapted from – The question of the trade, carrying and use of small arms and light weapons in the context of human rights and humanitarian norms, Working paper submitted by Ms. Barbara Frey in accordance with Sub-Commission decision 2001/120, E/CN.4/Sub.2/2002/39, 30 May 2002

Notes

1. This report adopts the definition of small arms and light weapons used in the 1997 report of the UN Panel of Governmental Experts on Small Arms (A/52/298, annex).

2. International Committee of the Red Cross, *Arms Availability and the Situation of Civilians in Armed Conflict (ICRC Arms Availability Report)*, Geneva, 1999, p.13

3. 'Going to the Source of the Illness', Dr Olive Kobusingye, presentation at 'Small Arms and the Humanitarian Community: Developing A Strategy for Action', Nairobi, Kenya, 18-20 November 2001.

4. Agreed to by the world's governments at a summit in 2000, the Millennium Development Goals commit governments to a set of clear targets aiming at a reduction in poverty and improvement in living standards for the world's poor.

5. US$87bn was spent by these regions over the last four years for which data are available. 'International Finance Facility' proposal, January 2003, HM Treasury, available from www.hm-treasury.gov.uk/documents/international_issues/global_new_deal/int_gnd_iff2003.cfm

6. *We the Peoples: the role of the UN in the 21st Century*, page 52, Millennium Report to the United Nations General Assembly.

7. Speech to Afghan people via Afghan radio, reported by the BBC, 9 January 2002 http://news.bbc.co.uk/1/hi/world/monitoring/media_reports/1752038.stm

8. *SIPRI Yearbook 2002: Armaments, Disarmament and International Security*, Stockholm International Peace Research Institute, Oxford University Press, 2002.

9. *Cost of the War – Economic, Social and Human Cost of the War in Sri Lanka*, January 2001, National Peace Council of Sri Lanka.

10. *Terror Trade Times*, issue no. 3 (AI Index: ACT 31/001/2002), Amnesty International.

11. *Hidden Scandal, Secret Shame – the Torture and Ill-treatment of Children* (AI Index: ACT 76/005/2000), Amnesty International.

12. Reports received by Amnesty International from 1995 onwards. Arms supplies to the DRC have also been linked to the exploitation of natural resources – see the Panel of Experts on the Illegal Exploitation of Natural Resources and Other Forms of Wealth of the Democratic Republic of the Congo, 16 October 2002 (S/2002/1146).

13. Amnesty International mission to Kisangani, November 2001.

14. Atti Parlamentari, Doc CVIII, Roma, Camera dei Deputati - Senato della Repubblica anni 1991-2001, www.irestoscana.it.

15. 'Rival Afghan commanders talk disarmament in restive north', Chris Otton, AFP, 20 July 2002 – from www.reliefweb.int.

16. 'The global menace of local strife', *The Economist*, 24 May 2003.

17. *Ending Violence Against Women: A Challenge for Development and Humanitarian Work*, Francine Pickup with Suzanne Williams and Caroline Sweetman, Oxford, Oxfam GB, 2001.

18. *Development Held Hostage: Assessing the effects of small arms on human development*, Robert Muggah, Peter Batchelor, April 2002, UN Development Programme (UNDP).

19. *Violence and Crime in Cross-national Perspective* 1900-1974, Dane Archer, Rosemary Gartner, Ann Arbor, USA, 1994.

20. *Stray Bullets: the Impact of Small Arms Misuse in Central America*, op. cit., p. 22.

21. Information provided by the Guatemalan National Civil Police.

22. *ICRC Arms Availability Report*, op.cit.

23. Oxfam, February 2001.

24. *Small Arms Survey 2002*, op. cit., p. 99.

25. Amnesty International, *The Wire*, March 2003 Vol 33 No 02 (AI Index: NWS 21/002/2003) and Amnesty International unpublished research information, February 2003; 'New World for Police Chief', Alex Spillius, 13 July 2003, www.smh.com.au

26. *Small Arms in the Pacific*, Philip Alpers and Conor Twyford, March 2003, Small Arms Survey Occasional Paper No 8.

27. *Child Combatants in Organised Armed Violence*, Viva Rio, Brazil.

28. SIM/DATASUS, IBGE, published in The Map of Violence, III, Jacobo Waiselfisz, UNESCO, Instituto Ayrton Senna, Ministerio da Justiça/SEDH. Brasilia, 2002.

29. Data supplied by *Viva Rio/ISER* from work with the Rio de Janeiro authorities.

30. Oxfam, April 97

31. *Small Arms Survey 2002: Counting the Human Cost*, a project of the Graduate Institute of International Studies Geneva, Oxford University Press, 2002, pp. 63, 70, 82. 'Colombian rebels trade drugs for arms', *Financial Times*, Andrew Bounds and James Wilson, 8 May 2002.

32. Amnesty International unpublished research paper.

33. Oxfam, March 2000.

34. *Angola's War Economy*, Institute for Security Studies, South Africa, 2000.

35. Oxfam 2001; 'The Dunblane father who simply wants to stop the senseless killing in Africa', Anna Pukas, *Daily Express*, 21 March 2001.

36. *'Breaking God's commands': the destruction of childhood by the Lord's Resistance Army*, Amnesty International, (AI Index: AFR 59/001/1997).

37. In a fairly typical case, at the port of Trieste Italian police confiscated 40 Austrian-made rifles which had been sold by a Swiss arms dealer to four Yugoslav nationals resident in Switzerland. See *Die Presse*, 20 May 1999, p. 4.

38. Dimevski, Sasko 'Macedonia – an illegal UCK arms depot?', *Skopje Utrinski Vesnik*, 13 September 1999, p. 5.

39. 'Israel and the Occupied Territories: Surviving under siege: The impact of movement restrictions on the right to work' September 2003, Amnesty International, AI Index MDE 15/001/203.

40. 'Israel's history of bomb blasts', BBC website, 11 June, 2003, http://news.bbc.co.uk/1/hi/world/middle_east/1197051.stm

41 *Terror Trade Times*, Amnesty International, June 2001.

42 US Customs statistics on arms exports, 1995-1999.

43 Oxfam interview, February 2003.

44 'Justice and force in postwar Iraq', Simon Apiku, World Press Review, 16 June 2003, www.worldpress.org/Mideast/1200.cfm.

45 *Explosive Remnants of War – unexploded ordnance and post conflict communities,* Landmine Action, April 2002.

46 Heidelberg Institute for International Conflict Research (HIIK), 2002, Conflict Barometer 2002, www.hiik.de/en/main.htm

47 For a summary of these rules, see Amnesty International's *10 Basic Human Rights Standards for Law Enforcement Officials* (AI Index: POL 30/004/1998).

48 'Policing to protect human rights – A survey of police practice in the countries of the Southern African Development Community 1997-2002', Amnesty International (AI Index: AFR 03/004/2002).

49 *Terror Trade Times*, issue no. 4, Amnesty International, May 2003.

50 'Diagnóstico sobre la situación actual de las armas ligeras y violencia en Guatemala', Mario Rodriguez, 2000.

51 *Stray Bullets: the Impact of Small Arms Misuse in Central America*, William Godnick, Robert Muggah, Camilla Waszink, October 2002; Small Arms Survey, occasional paper no. 5, p. 15.

52 *Small Arms Survey 2001: Profiling the Problem*, a project of the Graduate Institute of International Studies Geneva, Oxford University Press, 2001, pp. 17, 62.

53 *Reconsidering the Tools of War: Small Arms and Humanitarian Action*, Robert Muggah, Martin Griffiths, Humanitarian Practice Network Paper 39, July 2002.

54 *Small Arms Survey 2002*, op. cit., p. 79.

55 Ibid., p. 14.

56 Kalashnikov: 'I wish I'd made a lawnmower', *Guardian* (UK), 30 July 2002. www.guardian.co.uk/international/story/0,3604,765355,00.html.

57 *Small Arms Survey 2001* op. cit., p. 102, plus current population figures.

58 'Annan keeps pressure on US for Liberia role', David Clarke, Reuters, 30 June 2003, http://story.news.yahoo.com/news?tmpl=story&cid=578&ncid=578&e=9&u=/nm/20030630/ts_nm/liberia_dc.

59 *Small Arms Survey 2001*, op. cit., p. 208.

60 Dr. Joseph P. Smaldone, *Arms and Conflict in Africa: Links and Levers,* 2001; also Cassady Craft, *Weapons for Peace, Weapons for War: The effect of arms transfers on War Outbreak, Involvement and Outcomes*, 1999.

61 *Rwanda: Arming the Perpetrators of the Genocide* (AI Index: AFR 02/014/1995), Amnesty International; *Rwanda/Zaire: Rearming with Impunity: International Support for the Perpetrators of the Rwandan Genocide*, Human Rights Watch, May 1995; *Arming Rwanda: The Arms Trade and Human Rights Abuses in the Rwandan War,* Human Rights Watch Short Report, vol. 6, no. 1, January 1994. A detailed review of the evidence is contained in *The Arms Fixers*,

Chapter 3, Brian Wood and Johan Peleman (NISAT, 1999), including papers from the archive of the former Rwanda Ministry of Defence found in eastern Zaire in November 1996; the six reports published by the UN International Commission of Inquiry established pursuant to Resolution 1013 (1995) of the UN Security Council, to 'investigate, inter alia, reports relating to the sale or supply of arms and related materiel to former Rwandan government forces in the Great Lakes region in violation of Council Resolution 918, 997 and 1011'; and the Report of the French Parliamentary commission of inquiry into France's role before and during the Rwanda genocide, 15 December 1998.

62 Ed Cairns, Oxfam: internal document on conflict resolution.

63 *The Key to Peace: Unlocking the Human Potential of Sudan*, Interagency paper, Save the Children, Christian Aid, Oxfam, CARE, IRC, Tearfund, May 2002.

64 *A Catalogue of Failures: G8 Arm Exports and Human Rights Violations* (AI Index: IOR 30/003/2003), Amnesty International

65 'Hail of cluster bombs leaves a trail of death', Robert Fisk, *The Independent*, 3 April 2003.

66 *Small Arms Survey 2001*, op. cit. Also Wendy Cukier, 'Firearms regulation: Canada in the international context', *Chronic Diseases in Canada*, April 1998, www.hc-sc.gc.ca/pphb-dgspsp/publicat/cdic-mcc/19-1/d_e.html. See also M Miller, D Azrael, and D. Hemenway, 'Rates of household firearm ownership and homicide across US regions and states, 1988-1997', *American Journal of Public Health*, 1 December 2002, Vol. 92, Issue 12.

67 Peter Cummings, Thomas D. Koepsell, 'Does owning a firearm increase or decrease the risk of death?', *Controversies*, 5 August 1998, JAMA; and Matthew Miller, David Hemenway, 'Firearm prevalence and the risk of suicide: a review', *Harvard Health Policy Review*, Vol. 2 No. 2, Fall 2001; and 'Rates of homicide, suicide, and firearm-related death among children – 26 industrialized countries', *MMWR (Morbidity and Mortality Weekly Report)*, Vol. 46, No. 5, 7 February 1997, pp. 101-5; and Matthew Miller, Deborah Azrael, David Hemenway, 'Firearm availability and unintentional firearm deaths, suicide, and homicide among 5-14 year olds', *The Journal of Trauma*, Vol. 52, No. 2, 2002.

68 *Brazil: Vote to Protect Human Rights in Brazil – Agesandro da Costa Pereira* (AI Index: AMR 19/019/2002), Amnesty International.

69 'Forgotten victims; the full human cost of US air strikes will never be known, but many more died than those killed directly by bombs' Jonathan Steele, *Guardian*,20 May 2002.

70 Robert Muggah and Peter Batchelor, *Development Held Hostage: Assessing the effects of small arms on human development*, UNDP, April 2002.

71 Magdalene Hsien Chen Pua (ed.), *The Devastating Impact of Small Arms and Light Weapons on the Lives of Women; a collection of testimonies*, IANSA, http://peacewomen.org/campaigns/international/iansawomen/testimoniesiansa.pdf; and *The Impact of Small Arms on Health, Human Rights and Development in Medellín: A Case Study*, Oxfam, January 2000.

72 Amnesty International memorandum to the UN Security Council: Appeal for a commission of inquiry to investigate reports of atrocities in eastern Zaire, 24 March 1997 (AI Index 62/011/1997).

73 'Murdered with impunity, the street children who live and die like vermin', *Guardian Newspapers*, 28 May 2003, www.buzzle.com/editorials/5-28-2003-40914.asp

74 Richard Horton, 'Croatia and Bosnia: the imprints of war – I: consequences', *Lancet* 1999, 353: 2139-44.

75 Paul B Spiegel and Peter Salama, 'War and mortality in Kosovo, 1998-99: an epidemiological testimony', *Lancet* 2000, 355: 2204-9.

76 Michael Fleshman, *Small arms in Africa, Counting the cost of gun violence*, www.un.org/ecosocdev/geninfo/afrec/vol15no4/154arms.htm.

77 *Child Combatants in Organized Armed Violence: a study of children and adolescents involved in territorial drug faction disputes in Rio de Janeiro*, Luke Dowdney, ISER and Viva Rio, first edition for seminar, 9 September 2002.

78 Ibid.

79 *Burundi: Poverty, isolation and ill-treatment – Juvenile Justice in Burundi* (AI Index: AFR 16/011/2002), Amnesty International.

80 Take a Step to Stamp Out Torture (AI Index: ACT 40/013/2000), Amnesty International.

81 *Combating Torture: a manual for action* (AI Index: ACT 40/001/2003), Amnesty International.

82 Meredith Turshen, 'The political economy of rape', *Victims, Perpetrators or Actors? Gender, Armed Conflict and Political Violence*, Caroline O.N. Moser and Fiona C. Clark (eds.), London: Zed Books, 2001.

83 The incidence of rape in Rwanda has been reported much higher, but this is the figure supplied by WHO in 2000. 'The political economy of rape', op. cit. See also 'Croatia and Bosnia: the imprints of war - I. Consequences', op. cit.

84 *Soldiers score own goal in war on AIDS*, Africa Health, 14 November 2002

85 *Ending Violence Against Women: A Challenge for Development and Humanitarian Work*, op. cit.

86 'Gender and Small Arms', Wendy Cukier, Small Arms Firearms Education and Research Network (SAFER-Net), www.ryerson.ca/SAFER-Net/.

87 *Ending Violence Against Women: A Challenge for Development and Humanitarian Work*, op. cit.

88 Examples in this paragraph are cited in Wendy Cukier, 'Gender and Small Arms', op. cit.

89 *Ending Violence Against Women: A Challenge for Development and Humanitarian Work*, op. cit.

90 'Croatia and Bosnia: the imprints of war - I. Consequences', op. cit.

91 Elisabeth Rehn and Ellen Johnson Sirleaf, *Women, War and Peace*, UNIFEM, 2002.

92 'Croatia and Bosnia: the imprints of war - I. Consequences', op. cit.

93 Ibid.

94 Survey undertaken by the Palestinian Ministry of Social Affairs. From 'The lost children of Rafah', *Observer* magazine, 9 February 2003.

95 Oxfam Philippines team, 2003.

96 *World Refugee Survey 2003*, US Committee for Refugees, May 2003 .

97 For statistics relevant to gender and age, see UNHCR *Statistical Yearbook 2001*, October 2002.

98 *World Refugee Survey 2003*, op. cit.

99 *The Key to Peace: Unlocking the Human Potential of Sudan*, op. cit.

100 Submission to UK and Irish governments in advance of the 59th UN Commission on Human Rights, from ABColombia, UK, and Irish NGOs working in Colombia (CAFOD, Christian Aid, Oxfam, Save the Children UK, SCIAF, Trocaire), February 2003.

101 *Guinea and Sierra Leone: No place of refuge*, Amnesty International, October 2001, AI Index: AFR 05/06/2001.

102 Testimony given to Amnesty International at transit camps outside Freetown in March 2001.

103 *Asylum Applications Lodged in Industrialized Countries: Levels and Trends, 2000-2002*, UNHCR, March 2003.

104 See 'Afghanistan: International responsibility for human rights disaster' (AI Index: ASA 11/009/1995), Amnesty International; *A Catalogue of Failures: G8 arms exports and human rights violations*, op. cit.; and 'Turkey: no security without human rights' (AI Index: EUR 44/084/1996), Amnesty International; and *The Arms Fixers*, op. cit., chapter 2.

105 Oxfam GB, June 2000.

106 'Combat AIDS: HIV and the world's armed forces', *Healthlink Worldwide*, 2002.

107 'Report says civilians targeted by government and affiliated militias', IRIN report, 11 February 2003.

108 *Amnesty International, Annual Report 2003* (AI Index: POL 10/003/2003).

109 Amelia Gentleman, 'Kremlin admits hundreds missing in Chechnya', *Guardian*, 5 June 2001; Last Seen ... : *Continued 'Disappearances' in Chechnya*, Human Rights Watch, April 2002; *The Russian Federation: Denial of justice* (AI Index: EUR 46/027/2002), Amnesty International.

110 *Human rights crisis in Kosovo Province: 'Disappeared' and 'missing' persons*, op. cit.

111 Report of the UN High Commissioner for Human Rights on the human rights situation in Colombia, 24 February 2003, E/CN.4/2003/13, p. 30.

112 See Amnesty International website http://web.amnesty.org/ai.nsf/countries/zimbabwe?OpenView&Start=1&Count=30&Expandall

113 *International Herald Tribune* 10.10.2002, p.6.

114 *Cost of the War – Economic,, Social and Human Cost of the War in Sri Lanka*, op. cit..

115 Figures from 2000 – Net ODA US$ 1,731 million; military spend US$ 1,686 million. This figure for military spending is less than the actual amount, because much military spending is not included in national figures.

116 'Paying the Ultimate Price: Analysis of the deaths of humanitarian aid workers (1997-2001)', Dennis King, consultant, UN Office for Coordination of Humanitarian Affairs 15 January 2002; Sheik Mani et al., 'Deaths among humanitarian workers', *British Medical Journal*, Vol. 321, pp. 166-8, 15 July 2000.

117 'Time is Running Out: the Humanitarian Situation in Afghanistan', Oxfam Briefing Note, 17 October 2001.

118 'Under Fire: the Human Cost of Small Arms in North-east Democratic Republic of the Congo: A Case Study', Oxfam, January 2001.

119 *Stray Bullets: the Impact of Small Arms Misuse in Central America*, op. cit., p. 31.

120 Discussion with Benedict Peter Chacha, Foundation Help, at Nairobi workshop, October 2002.

121 *Human Development Report 2002*, UNDP, www.hdr.undp.org/reports/global/2002/en/.

122 *The Impact of Small Arms on Health, Human Rights and Development in Medellín: a Case Study*, Oxfam, January 2003.

123 'Going to the Source of the Illness', Dr Olive Kobusingye, presentation at 'Small Arms and the Humanitarian Community: Developing A Strategy for Action', Nairobi, Kenya, 18-20 November 2001.

124 *Under Fire: the Human Cost of Small Arms in North-east Democratic Republic of the Congo: A Case Study*, op. cit.

125 'Iraqis loot, create chaos', *The Associated Press*, 12 April 2003. www.thehollandsentinel.net/stories/041203/new_041203026.shtm.

126 *Women, War and Peace*, op. cit.

127 'Going to the Source of the Illness', op. cit.

128 'Croatia and Bosnia: the imprints of war - I. Consequences', op. cit.

129 Miriam Abramovay and Maria das Graças, Violência nas escolas, Brasília, UNESCO (2002).

130 Robert Muggah and Peter Batchelor, *Development Held Hostage: Assessing the Effects of Small Arms on Human Development*, UNDP, April 2002, p. 30.

131 *Violência nas escolas*, op.cit.

132 US$87bn was spent by these regions over the last four years for which data is available. It is estimated that the education goal requires US$10bn a year extra and the maternal mortality goal requires US$12bn a year extra. See 'International Finance Facility' proposal, January 2003, HM Treasury, available from www.hm-treasury.gov.uk/documents/international_issues/global_new_deal/int_gnd_iff2003.cfm.

133 Oxfam – November 2002.

134 Millennium Development Goals website: www.developmentgoals.org/index.html.

135 Dan Smith, *Atlas of War and Peace*, Earthscan, London, 2003.

136 'Foreign Report', Jane's Information Group, posted on website, 13 August 2002.

137 Hannah Galvin, 'The impact of defence spending on the economic growth of developing countries: a cross-section study', *Defence and Peace Economics*, Vol. 14, No. 1/2003; Carlos P. Barros, 'Development and conflict in the Balkans: catchup and military expenditure', Defence and Peace Economics, Vol. 13, No. 5/2002.

138 In the USA this has not been proven: Michael P. Gerace, 'US military expenditures and economic growth: some evidence from spectral methods', *Defence and Peace Economics*, Vol. 13, No. 1/2002. In Greece, increasing military expenditure has been linked with declining profitability: Christos Kollias, Thanasis Maniatis, 'Military expenditure and the profit rate in Greece', *Defence and Peace Economics*, Vol. 14, No. 2/2003. In Turkey, military expenditure is linked with unemployment: Julide Yildirim, Selami Sezgin, 'Military expenditure and employment in Turkey', *Defence and Peace Economics*, Vol. 14, No. 2/2003.

139 Paul Dunne, Sam Perlo Freeman, *The Impact of a Responsible Arms Control Policy on the UK Economy*, November 2002, commissioned by Oxfam, publication forthcoming.

140 'The global menace of local strife', *The Economist*, 24 May 2003.

141 Of the 12 countries which have a high defence burden, with more than five per cent of their GDP dedicated to military expenditure, five, including the top two, are defined by the UNDP as having low human development; according to 'Human Development Indicators 2002', from UNDP website, checked by author January 2003. http://stone.undp.org/hdr/reports/global/2002/en/indicator/indicator.cfm?File=index_indicators.html.

142 See www.ecaar.org/Newsletter/May03/ellis.htm and other work by Terry Crawford-Browne.

143 In South Africa, a realistic current estimate for the cost of a course of generic HIV/AIDS combination therapy is around US$ 600 per year. According to UNAIDS 2002, there are five million HIV-positive South Africans.

144 A report from the International Civil Aviation Organization, commissioned by the World Bank, stated that a more appropriate system could be bought for one tenth of the price.

145 *World Report on Violence and Health 2002*. Edited by Etienne G. Krug, Linda Dahlberg, James A. Mercy, Anthony B. Zwi and Rafael Lozano.

146 *Cost of the War – Economic, Social and Human Cost of the War in Sri Lanka*, op. cit.

147 The Regional Adviser for Emergency and Humanitarian Action at the WHO Regional Office for Africa, Dr Komla Siamevi, speaking at a meeting in Brazzaville, reported by IRIN, 'Africa: Wars costing US$15 billion per year', 13 March 2003.

148 Macartan Humphreys, *Economics and Violent Conflict*, Harvard University, August 2002. www.preventconflict.org/portal/economics/Essay.pdf.

149 Internal Oxfam briefing paper on Iraq, 2002.

150 Peter Chalk, 'Light arms trading in SE Asia', *Jane's Intelligence Review*, 1 March 2001.

151 'The Dunblane father who simply wants to stop the senseless killing in Africa', op. cit.

152 President Bush's remarks at the White House ceremony to honour victims of the September 11 2001 attacks, The White House, Washington, DC, 11 March 2002. http://usinfo.state.gov/products/pubs/sixmonths/bushremarks.htm.

153 'Stop arms to human rights abusers! Defend the Leahy Law', Amnesty International USA website www.amnestyusa.org/stoparms/history.html

154 *SIPRI Yearbook 2002: Armaments, Disarmament and International Security*, op. cit. According to one study by the International Institute for Strategic Studies, the total spending in 1997 alone on defence by the Saudi Arabian government was estimated at US$ 18.2 billion.

155 *Amnesty International Report 2002* (AI Index: POL 10/001/2002), Uzbekistan entry, pp. 261-2. Amnesty International received reports throughout 2001 that devout Muslim prisoners were singled out for particularly cruel, inhuman, or degrading treatment in places of detention.

156 *Amnesty International Reports 2001, 2002 and 2003*. On abuses during the East Timor crisis, see *Indonesia: Paying the price for 'stability'* (AI Index: ASA 21/001/1998), Amnesty International.

157 'Ministers back 20-fold rise in arms sales to Indonesia', *Guardian*, 1 July 2003.

158 Report of the UN High Commissioner for Human Rights on the Human Rights Situation in Colombia, 24 February 2003, E/CN.4/2003/13.

159 Tamar Gabelnick, 'New Supplemental Bill will make the world safe for oil, but not safe for US', *Foreign Policy in Focus*, 18 June 2002.

160 'Sweeping military aid under the anti-terrorism rug: security assistance post September 11th', *Arms Sales Monitor*, No 48, Federation of American Scientists, http://fas.org/asmp/library/asm/asm48.html. *United States: Dangerous Dealings: Changes to US military assistance after September 11th*, Human Rights Watch, February 2002.

161 *Legitimacy and Legality, Key Issues in the Fight against Terrorism*, Loretta Bondi, 9 November 2002, Fund for Peace.

162 *Uzbekistan: US Rubber Stamps Human Rights*, Human Rights Watch, 9 September 2002, http://hrw.org/press/2002/09/uzbek0909.htm.

163 Jean-Marc Mojon, 'Israel's arms industry cashes in on new markets, new technologies', Agence France-Presse, 22 May 2003.

164 Includes deals to Oman, Turkey, Jordan, UAE, Saudi Arabia, and Kuwait. Peter Baker, 'Iraq's neighborhood thick with US arms; weapons and technology traded for support', *Washington Post*, 5 February 2003.

165 *Transfers of major conventional weapons to Iraq 1973-2002*, SIPRI, http://projects.sipri.se/armstrade/Trnd_Ind_IRQ_Imps_73-02.pdf.

166 Michael Dobbs, 'US had key role in Iraq buildup', *Washington Post*, 30 December 2002. See also *A Catalogue of Failures: G8 Arms Exports and Human Rights Violations*, op. cit.

167 Calvin Woodward, 'A market where demand is high – many nations are competing to sell military hardware', Associated Press, 12 December 2002.

168 Chris Brummitt, 'Indonesia resumes war with Aceh rebels, but at what cost?', Associated Press, 26 May 2003.

169 Injuries are measured in DALYs (disability-adjusted life-years). One DALY is one lost year of healthy life. C. Murray and A. Lopez, eds., 'The global burden of disease: a comprehensive assessment of mortality and disability from diseases, injuries, and risk factors in 1990 and projected to 2020', Harvard School of Public Health on behalf of the WHO and the World Bank, 1996 (*Global Burden of Disease and Injury Series*, vol. I).

170 Security Council statement, 17 March 2003 http://www.un.org/News/Press/docs/2003/sc7686.doc.htm

171 'War and mortality in Kosovo, 1998-99: an epidemiological testimony', op. cit.

172 UN Panel of Experts Report on Liberia, October 2001.

173 Ibid.

174 Uganda Civil Aviation Authorities; other data provided by the International Peace Information Service, Antwerp, 2002.

175 UN Report of the Panel of Experts pursuant to Security Council resolution 1343 (2001), paragraph 19, concerning Liberia, October 2001.

176 *The Terror Trade Times*, issue no. 4, op. cit. According to UN investigators, at the time of writing this report the trial of Sanjivan Ruprah was still continuing.

177 Oxfam – April 2001.

178 *Arming Rwanda: The Arms Trade and Human Rights Abuses in the Rwandan War*, op. cit.

179 *The Arms Fixers*, op. cit., Chapter 3.

180 Michael Renner, *The Anatomy of Resource Wars*, Worldwatch paper 162, October 2002. This author additionally points out that more than 5 million people were killed in the 1990s, almost 6 million fled to neighbouring countries, and between 11 million and 15 million were internally displaced.

181 'Les Suspects Habituels: les Armes et les Mercenaires du Liberia en Côte d'Ivoire et en Sierra Leone', Global Witness, March 2003 .

182 *Marketing the New 'Dogs of War'*, International Consortium of Investigative Journalists, published on the Internet by the Centre for Public Integrity, November 2002, www.publicintegrity.org/dtaweb/icij_bow.asp.

183 Deborah Avant, *The Market for Force*, manuscript chapter 2, book forthcoming 2003.

184 *Unmatched Power, Unmet Principles: the Human Rights Dimensions of US Training of Foreign Military and Police Forces*, op.cit.

185 *Cost of the War – Economic, Social and Human Cost of the War in Sri Lanka*, op. cit.

186 *Small Arms Survey 2001*, op. cit.

187 'Shooting enforces Midlands fear factor', BBC website, 4 January 2003, http://news.bbc.co.uk/1/hi/england/2627331.stm

188 Personal communication – Jessica Galleria, Viva Rio, Brazil.

189 Neil MacFarquhar, 'Yemen turns to tribes to aid hunt for Qaeda', *New York Times*, 27 October 2002.

190 BICC Conversion Survey 2002: *Global Disarmament, Demilitarisation and Demobilization*, Bonn International Center for Conversion, Baden-Baden. 'Traditional Cultural Practices and Small Arms in the Middle East: Problems and Solutions', workshop report, November 2002, Jordan Institute of Diplomacy.

191 'The Dunblane father who simply wants to stop the senseless killing in Africa', op. cit.

192 'Small Arms Global Reach Uproots Tribal Traditions', Karl Vick, *Washington Post*, 8 July 2001.

193 F. Mohamed F., speaking at the CODEP 'Beyond Working in Conflict' workshop at Oxford Brookes University, 4–6 November 1996, quoted by Judith Large, 'Disintegration conflicts and the restructuring of masculinity', *Men and Masculinity*, Caroline Sweetman (ed.), Oxfam, Oxford, 1997, p.23.

194 *The Impact of Small Arms on Health, Human Rights and Development in Medellín: A Case Study*, op. cit.

195 Suzanne Williams, quoted in Francine Pickup with Suzanne Williams and Caroline Sweetman, *Ending Violence Against Women: A Challenge for Development and Humanitarian Work*, op. cit., p.146.

196 Research done by Tsuma William in 2001, personal communication 2002.

197 *The State of the World's Children*, UNICEF, 2002, p 42.

198 The United Nations Convention of the Rights of the Child regards anyone under 18 years of age as a child.

199 Amy Kazmin, 'Burma "forcing children into army"', *Financial Times* (London), 16 October 2002.

200 Sandra Jordan, 'El Salvador's teenage beauty queens live and die by gang law: the abandoned children who find power, glory – and death – in violent street culture', *Observer* (London), 10 November 2002.

201 *Child Combatants in Organized Armed Violence: a study of children and adolescents involved in territorial drug faction disputes in Rio de Janeiro*, op. cit.

202 Alberto Concha-Eastman, PAHO regional advisor on violence, at Pan-American Health Organization meeting: 'Violence in the Americas, Alarming but Preventable', Washington DC, 12 June 2003.

203 *Small Arms Survey 2002*, op. cit. p.104.

204 Quoted in Small Arms in the Pacific, Philip Alpers and Conor Twyford, March 2003, Small Arms Survey Occasional Paper No 8.

205 Personal communication: Jessica Galeria, *Viva Rio*, Brazil, December 2002.

206 *Small Arms Survey 2002*, op. cit., pp. 104 and 97.

207 Spyros Demetriou, *Politics from the Barrel of a Gun: small arms proliferation and conflict in the Republic of Georgia (1989-2001)*, Small Arms Survey Occasional Paper No. 6, p.16, November 2002.

208 'Justice and force in postwar Iraq', op. cit. www.worldpress.org/Mideast/1200.cfm.

209 Oxfam field trip, October 2002.

210 Pastoralism may be defined as a livelihood and culture which is dependent on the herding of livestock in areas where rainfall is too erratic to grow crops. The Pokot and Marakwet combine pastoralism with agriculture.

211 Joseph Ngala, 'Women key to disarmament', MS-Kenya, *Partner NEWS*, Vol. 4, No. 2, 2001, http://kenya.ms.dk/partnernews/visartikel.asp?id=188.

212 Anna Leer, 'Making sense of war zone Isiolo', MS-Kenya, *Partner NEWS*, Vol. 4, No. 2, 2001.

213 'First quarterly statistics update shows crime rate remains stable as fear of crime drops', UK Home Office press release, 9 January 2003, http://213.121.214.245/n_story.asp?item_id=330.

214 Fiona Brookman and Mike Maguire, *Reducing Homicide: Summary of a Review of the Possibilities*, RDS Occasional Paper no. 84, January 2003.

215 Information provided by the UK police, May 2003.

216 From website of Gun Free South Africa, updated May 2002, checked by author January 2003, www.gca.org.za/facts/statistics.htm, plus Crime Information Analysis Centre – South African Police Service, checked January 2003, www.saps.org.za/8_crimeinfo/200111/crime/illpos.htm

217 Dick Dahl, 'Hike in Gang Gun Violence Raises Old Concerns Anew', 24 January /2003, www.jointogether.org/gv/news/features/reader/0,2061,5562 32,00.html.

218 Dr Domitilla Sagramoso, 'The Proliferation of Illegal Small Arms and Light Weapons in and around the European Union', Saferworld and Center for Defence Studies, July 2001.

219 *Stray Bullets: the Impact of Small Arms Misuse in Central America*, op. cit., p.vii.

220 *Small Arms Survey*, 2002, op. cit.

221 Statement at 'Third Caribbean-United Kingdom Forum', Georgetown, April 2002.

222 *Child Combatants in Organized Armed Violence: a study of children and adolescents involved in territorial drug faction disputes in Rio de Janeiro*..

223 American National Center for Health Statistics, 1981-1999.

224 'The global menace of local strife', *The Economist*, 24 May 2003.

225 'Thai police seize arms cache destined for Indonesian rebels', Agence France-Presse, 15 July 2002; Edward Tang, 'Golden Triangle now a haven for terror arms', The Straits Times (Singapore), 4-9-2002.

226 *Thailand: Extrajudicial killing is not the way to suppress drug trafficking* (AI Index: ASA 39/001/2003), Amnesty International.

227 'Hike in Gang Gun Violence Raises Old Concerns Anew', op. cit.

228 Oxfam, April 2001.

229 *Conventional arms transfers to developing nations, 1994-2001*', op. cit., states that the average value of arms sales to developing countries for the period 1998 to 2001 was US$21.7bn; OECD website, www.oecd.org/xls/M00037000/M00037874.xls, for same period states net ODA was US$18.8bn. However, in 2001, arms exports were worth about half the total volume of aid.

230 T. J. Milling, 'Guns in America Part II; Killers, gang bangers and drug dealers go for their guns', *Houston Chronicle*, 1997, www.chron.com/content/chronicle/nation/guns/part2/gunscrime.html.

231 *Conventional Arms Transfers to Developing Nations*, 1994-2001, op. cit.

232 'Corruption in the Official Arms Trade', Policy Research Paper 001, April 2002, Catherine Courtney, Transparency International (UK)...

233 This is explicitly stated in the Department for Trade and Industry's Defence Industrial Policy of 2002 which also makes a strong case for the support of the industry through helping it export, www.dti.gov.uk/aerospace/policy.htm

234 Chalmers, M., Davies, N.V., Hartley, K. and Wilkinson, C. (2002): "The economic costs and benefits of UK defence exports", *Fiscal Studies*, Vol. 23, No. 3, September, pp 305-342.

235 It should also be pointed out that the short-term costs can be minimised, and long-term benefits maximised, by government efforts to re-train redundant defence workers and support demand and investment in affected regions.

236 Dunne, P., and Perlo Freeman, S., "The Impact of a Responsible Arms Control Policy on the UK Economy", report prepared for Oxfam, March 2003.

237 *The Terror Trade Times*, issue No. 4, op. cit.

238 Marco Garrido, *Small Arms Availability in the Philippines*, December 2002.

239 *A Catalogue of Failures: G8 arms exports and human rights violations*, op. cit.

240 Extensive trend analysis of available published data covering the four decades between 1960 and 1999, conducted by the UK-based Omega Foundation.

241 Mahamadou Nimaga, 'Study on the Problem of Small Arms in Mali – examples of Bamako, Gao and Nioro du Sahel', report commissioned by Oxfam, to be published in 2003.

242 *Stray Bullets: the Impact of Small Arms Misuse in Central America*, op. cit. Dr W James Arputharaj, Crisis in South Asia: humanity's number one killer – small arms, SAP (South Asia Partnership) International, 11 February 2003.

243 Scott Wilson, 'State of emergency, new taxes are set by Colombia's leader: campaign against guerrillas to intensify', *Washington Post*, 13 August 2002.

244 Steve Rodan, 'Hamas deploys anti-tank rocket', *Jane's Defence Weekly*, 10 July 2002.

245 *The Impact of Small Arms on Health, Human Rights and Development in Medellín: a Case Study*, op. cit.

246 Karl Penhaul, 'Colombia rebels wheel out secret weapon in war: home-made tanks', Reuters, 1 April 1998; and Pete Abel, 'Manufacturing trends – globalising the source', *Running Guns, the Global Black Market in Small Arms*, Lora Lumpe (ed.), Zed Books, 2000.

247 Afi Yakubu, *Country Study: Craft production of small arms in Ghana*, FOSDA, 2002.

248 *Small Arms Survey 2001*, op. cit., p.145.

249 Speech by Dr Oscar Arias during the public signing of the Nobel Peace laureates' International Code of Conduct on Arms Transfers, New York City, 29 May 1997, Cathedral of Saint John the Divine.

250 From *The Presidential Campaign*, 1976, Part I: Jimmy Carter, quoted in 'The Role of US Arms Transfers in Human Rights Violations: Rhetoric Versus Reality', testimony by William D. Hartung, Director, Arms Trade Resource Center, before the Subcommittee on International Operations and Human Rights, House International Relations Committee, 7 March 2001.

251 'India drops arms export blacklist', BBC website, 28 October 2002, http://news.bbc.co.uk/1/hi/business/2367431.stm.

252 'Arms Trade, Human Rights, and European Union Enlargement: The Record of Candidate Countries', Human Rights Watch, 8 October 2002, www.hrw.org/backgrounder/arms/eu_briefing.htm.

253 *A Catalogue of Failures: G8 arms exports and human rights violations*, op. cit.

254 Testimony Before the Senate Armed Services Committee: Defense Strategy Review, given by Secretary of Defense Donald H. Rumsfeld and Chairman of the Joint Chiefs of Staff General Hugh Shelton, Washington DC, 21 June 2001, US Department of Defense Website. www.defenselink.mil/speeches/2001/s20010621-secdef2.html

255 International laws include the prohibition on the use, stockpiling, production, and transfer of anti-personnel landmines and control of four types of weapon 'deemed to be excessively injurious or to have indiscriminate effects' in the Convention on Certain Conventional Weapons of 1980.

256 These include the Wassenaar Arrangement, OSCE guidelines and the only controls on the proliferation of certain large conventional weapons (Conventional Armed Forces in Europe Treaty and Florence Agreement).

257 *A Catalogue of Failures: G8 arms exports and human rights violations*, op. cit.

258 Nigel Morris, 'Government accused of hypocrisy over arms sales to African states', *Independent*, 27 May 2003.

259 'Britain tightens arms exports to Israel', Ewen MacAskill in Jerusalem and Richard Norton-Taylor, *Guardian*, 23 August 2002.

260 *Running Guns, the Global Black Market in Small Arms*, op. cit.

261 From Omega Foundation – originally noted in *St Petersburg Times* 16 April 1999.

262 Caroline Iootty de Paiva Dias, *MERCOSUR: Harmonizing Laws for the Prevention of Illicit Firearms Transfers*, Viva Rio Working Paper no 1, January 2003.

263 Amnesty International research 2003

264 From a taped interview, 2000.

265 Mark Stevenson, 'Nicaraguan rifles find their way from police into hands of Latin American terrorist group', The Associated Press, 7 July 2002; 'Panama-Colombia cooperating in OAS probe of 3 nation arms scam', EFE News Service, 10 August 2002; Andrew Bounds and James Wilson, 'Colombian rebels trade drugs for arms', *Financial Times*, 8 May 2002; Kathia Martinez, 'OAS report blames Nicaragua for deal that allowed guns to end up with Colombian paramilitaries', The Associated Press, 21 January 2003; Hugh Dellios, 'Latin war surplus feeds deadly trade', *Chicago Tribune*, 24 January 2003.

[266] Brian Wood and Johan Peleman, *The Arms Fixers: Controlling the Brokers and Shipping Agents* (Norwegian Initiative on Small Arms, Oslo, and British-American Security Information Council, London), November 1999.

[267] See 'Eastern Europe's Arsenal on the Loose: Managing Light Weapons Flows to Conflict Zones', *BASIC Papers*, British-American Security Information Council, Number 26, May 1998. www.basicint.org/bpaper26.htm.

[268] Prime Minister's press conference, 10 Downing Street, 25 July 2002, see www.number10.gov.uk/output/Page3000.asp.

[269] Research undertaken by the Omega Foundation.

[270] *Out of Control, the Loopholes in UK Controls of the Arms Trade*, Oxfam GB, December 1998.

[271] *A Catalogue of Failures: G8 arms exports and human rights violations*, op. cit., Chapters 4 and 6.

[272] Lora Lumpe, paper to Small Arms and the Humanitarian Community: Developing A Strategy for Action, Nairobi, Kenya - November 18-20, 2001

[273] *Impact of Small Arms on Health, Human Rights and Development in Medellín: A Case Study*, op. cit.

[274] Oxfam field trip to Zugdidi, Georgia, 2000.

[275] Impact of Small Arms on Health, Human Rights and Development in Medellín: A Case Study, op.cit.

[276] *Politics from the Barrel of a Gun: small arms proliferation and conflict in the Republic of Georgia* (1989-2001), op. cit.

[277] Adele Kirsten, Gun Free South Africa, speech to the UN conference to Prevent, Combat and Eradicate the Illicit Trade in Small Arms and Light Weapons in All Its Aspects, New York, July 2001.

[278] *Small Arms in the Pacific*, op. cit., p. 39; and *Solomon Islands: A Forgotten Conflict* (AI Index: ASA 43/005/2000), Amnesty International.

[279] Data on Brazilian and foreign-produced small arms seized by police and stockpiled at DFAE between 1950 and 2001, *Viva Rio* and Government of the State of Rio, July 2002.

[280] 'Alarm at illegal weapon sales to rogue states', *South China Morning Post*, 21 October 2002.

[281] 'Arming Saddam: The Yugoslav Connection', International Crisis Group report, 3 December 2002; 'Eastern Europe arms Saddam', Ian Traynor in Zagreb and Nicholas Wood in Belgrade, 25 November 2002, *Guardian*; 'Illegal weapons deals threaten Balkan status in NATO', *Deutsche Presse-Agentur*, 13 November 2002; 'The former Soviet republics are accused of supplying weapons to rogue states in defiance of United Nation or US embargoes', *Financial Times* (London), 21 October 2002, Robert Anderson, Stephen Fidler, Andrew Jack, Stefan Wagstyle, Tom Warner; 'Report: 3 Firms Sold Arms To Iraq', *The Moscow Times*, 20 December 2002, Alex Nicholson and Simon Saradzhyan; 'Bulgarian arms exports investigated', Elizabeth Konstantinova, Jane's Intelligence Review, 1 February 2003.

[282] *A Catalogue of Failures: G8 arms exports and human rights violations*, op. cit.; Jack Anderson and Joseph Spear, 'Greece sells US, Israeli arms to Iraq', *Newsday* (New York), 17 May 1988.

[283] 'US military stops giving confiscated arms to Afghan warlords', The Associated Press, 26 October 2002, Chris Hawley.

[284] Tanja Subotic, 'Seven years after the war, Bosnians still cling to their weapons', Agence France-Presse, 19 August 2002, www.reliefweb.int/w/rwb.nsf/s/39BAD28B5B1C0B6C85256 C1A00637C2F.

[285] Alban Bala, 'Balkan weapons roundup', Radio Free Europe/Radio Liberty, 15 April 2002, from www.reliefweb.int.

[286] 'The OSCE Draft Best Practice Guide on Small Arms and Light Weapons', Vienna, 9 January 2003. Also the Wassenaar Arrangement Best Practice Guidelines for the Exports of Small Arms and Light Weapons, adopted 11-12 December 2002. The Wassenaar Arrangement includes most of the world's significant exporters of conventional arms and 'dual use' goods.

[287] From foreword to *Small Arms Survey 2002*, op. cit.

[288] For more up-to-date information, check http://untreaty.un.org/English/TreatyEvent2003/index.htm.

[289] See UN document A/Conf.192/15.

[290] 'Guns in America Part II; Killers, gang bangers and drug dealers go for their guns', op. cit.

[291] Adapted from a classic definition of arms control by Thomas Schelling and Morton Halperin in 1961, quoted in SIPRI Yearbook 2002, op. cit.

[292] Yvonne E. Keairns, T*he Voices of Girl Child Soldiers, Summary*, Quaker UN Office, October 2002, www.afsc.org/quno/Resources/QUNOchildsoldiers.pdf.

[293] *Human Development Report 2002*, UNDP.

[294] Working paper submitted by Ms. Barbara Frey in accordance with Sub-Commission decision 2001/120, E/CN.4/Sub.2/2002/39, 30 May 2002.

[295] The core principles were first drafted by a group of Nobel Peace Laureates, led by Oscar Arias, and with legal and technical support was developed into the Arms Trade Treaty (ATT). Peace Laureates backing the ATT: American Friends Service Committee, Amnesty International, Oscar Arias, Norman Borlaug, His Holiness the Dalai Lama, John Hume, International Physicians for the Prevention of Nuclear War, Mairead Maguire, Rigoberta Menchu, Adolfo Perez Esquivel, Jose Ramos Horta, Joseph Rotblat, Aung San Suu Kyi, the Reverend Desmond Tutu, Lech Walesa, Elie Wiesel, Betty Williams, and Jody Williams.

[296] Emanuela Gillard, *What is Legal? What is Illegal? Limitations on Transfers of Small Arms under International Law*, Lauterpacht Research Centre for International Law, Cambridge, March 2001. The principle is stated in Article 16 of the International Law Commission's Articles on Responsibility of States for Internationally Wrongful Acts, adopted in 2001, in the following terms: 'A State which aids or assists another State in the commission of an internationally wrongful act by the latter is internationally responsible for doing so if: (a) that State does so with knowledge of the circumstances of the internationally wrongful act; (b) the act would be internationally wrongful if committed by that State.'

[297] See Table in Appendix.

[298] Arms Trade Treaty conference at Oxfam GB, Oxford, January 2003.

[299] Personal communication, Lisa Misol, Human Rights Watch, January 2003.

300 Annual Report: The Netherlands Arms Export Policy in 2001, Dutch Ministry of Economic Affairs, www.ez.nl/beleid/home_ond/handelspolitiek/pdf/Jaarrapport_2001_ENG.pdf

301 Contact the International Campaign to Ban Landmines: www.icbl.org.

302 'Small Arms and the Humanitarian Community: Developing A Strategy for Action', Nairobi, Kenya, November 18-20, 2001.

303 Section II, paragraph 11.

304 Civil Society Consultation on the ECOWAS Moratorium: Beyond the UN 2001 Conference, Rapporteur's Report, www.ecowas.int.

305 Those states that have ratified so far are Antigua and Barbuda (2003), Argentina (2001), Bahamas (1998), Belize (1997), Bolivia (1999), Brazil (1999), Colombia (2003), Costa Rica (2000), Ecuador (1999), El Salvador (1999), Grenada (2002), Guatemala (2003), Mexico (1998), Nicaragua (1999), Panama (1999), Paraguay (2000), Peru (1999), Saint Lucia (2003), Uruguay (2001) and Venezuela (2002).

306 This statement was given in the context of Mali's own disarmament as a prelude to the return of political stability and a renewal of economic development projects.

307 Oxfam, November 2000.

308 Control of arms brokering is referred to in several political agreements on small arms, notably the UN Programme of Action, the UN Firearms Protocol, and the SADC Firearms Protocol. In May 2003 the EU Member States also agreed to adopt a joint position on controlling arms brokering.

309 Ibid., p, 1.

310 United Nations International Study on Firearms Regulation, United Nations Publications, Sales No. E.98.XIV.2, pages 108-9.

311 See Working paper submitted by Ms. Barbara Frey, op. cit.

312 Article 3 of the Universal Declaration of Human Rights.

313 Article 6 of the International Covenant on Civil and Political Rights. See report by the Special Rapporteur on Extrajudicial, Summary and Arbitrary Executions which includes the requirement on states 'to take positive measures of a preventive and protective nature necessary to ensure the right to life of any person under its jurisdiction.' (E/CN.4/2001/9, para. 7).

314 For example, the UN Special Rapporteur on Violence against Women has affirmed that: 'a state can be held complicit where it fails systematically to provide protection from private actors who deprive any person of his/her human rights... To avoid such complicity, states must demonstrate due diligence by taking active measures to protect, prosecute and punish private actors who commit abuses.' Report by the UN Special Rapporteur on Violence against Women, E/CN.4/1996/53, paragraphs 32 and 33.

315 Interviews by Brian Wood with UK, South African, and Malawian police, 2000-2002.

316 The UN Basic Principles on the use of force and firearms by law enforcement officials.

317 For example, police in the UK are not normally issued with high-velocity assault rifles, and the civilian possession of firearms is strictly limited.

318 Brian Wood, with Undule Mwakasungura and Robert Phiri, Report of the Malawi Community Safety and Firearms Control Project, Lilongwe, August 2001.

319 Oxfam, October 2002.

320 Captain Pillay, Police Special Investigations Task Team, addressing 30 Amnesty International and local NGO representatives, Edendale, South Africa, April 2002.

321 Universal Declaration of Human Rights, adopted by UN General Assembly resolution 217A (111) of 10 December 1948.

322 International Covenant on Civil and Political Rights, Article 6(1): 'Every human being has the inherent right to life. This right shall be protected by law. No one shall be arbitrarily deprived of his life.' www.unhchr.ch/html/menu3/b/a_ccpr.htm.

323 UN Code of Conduct for Law Enforcement Officials, UN Basic Principles on the Use of Force and Firearms by Law Enforcement Officials. For a summary, see 10 Basic Human Rights Standards for Law Enforcement Officials (AI Index: POL 30/004/1998), Amnesty International.

324 The four Geneva Conventions of 1949 and their two Additional Protocols of 1977 are the principal instruments of international humanitarian law; the documents concerning the International Criminal Court reaffirm prohibition and define particular acts.